Art Weinstein, PhD

Defining Your Market
Winning Strategies
for High-Tech, Industrial,
and Service Firms

Defining Your Market

*Winning Strategies
for High-Tech, Industrial,
and Service Firms*

HAWORTH Marketing Resources
Innovations in Practice & Professional Services
William J. Winston, Senior Editor

New, Recent, and Forthcoming Titles:

Defining Your Market
Winning Strategies for High-Tech, Industrial, and Service Firms

Art Weinstein, PhD

The Haworth Press
New York • London

The Haworth Press, Inc., 10 Alice Street, Binghamton, NY 13904-1580

Cover design by Marylouise E. Doyle.

Library of Congress Cataloging-in-Publication Data

Weinstein, Art.
    Defining your market : winning strategies for high-tech, industrial, and service firms / Art Weinstein.
        p.   cm.
    Includes bibliographical references and index.
    ISBN 0-7890-0251-5 (alk. paper).
    1. Strategic planning. 2. Market share. 3. Industrial management. 4. High technology industries—Management. 5. Service industries—Management. I. Title.
HD30.28.W376   1998
658.8'02—dc21
                                                                                                98-12798
                                                                                                        CIP

ABOUT THE AUTHOR

Art Weinstein, PhD, is Professor of Marketing in the School of Business and Entrepreneurship at Nova Southeastern University in Fort Lauderdale, Florida. A nationally known researcher/writer on market definition and segmentation, Dr. Weinstein has provided consulting and training services to companies such as Hewlett-Packard and Intel and to government agencies, professional associations, and universities. He is the author of more than thirty journal articles and papers on marketing strategy issues and is the author of *Market Segmentation: Using Demographics, Psychographics, and Other Niche Marketing Techniques to Predict Customer Behavior,* Revised Edition (1994). Dr. Weinstein is also the founder and editor of the *Journal of Segmentation in Marketing: Innovations in Market Identification and Targeting* (The Haworth Press, Inc.). In addition, Dr. Weinstein is a member of the American Marketing Association and the Academy of Marketing Science.

CONTENTS

Preface

Market definition is the heart and soul of successful business strategy. Consider the remarkable success of BellSouth, Canon, Dell Computer, General Electric, Hewlett-Packard, Intel, Johnson & Johnson, Merck, Microsoft, and Southwest Airlines—these companies truly know their markets! Business executives often struggle with how to define the best markets for their companies, business units, and products. AT&T, CompuServe, IBM, Kodak, Motorola, and Xerox have had their share of ups and downs; and, Apple, Digital Equipment Corporation, General Motors, and Philips have suffered when they failed to understand their markets.

A few years ago, at one of my executive seminars on "Segmenting and Targeting Business Markets," a Fortune 500 company's vice president of marketing asked me a tough question. I recall it vividly. "Yes, segmentation is important and interesting, but how do we know if we have defined the right presegmented market for our business?" This critical query (how do we define markets?) resurfaced on many occasions in consulting engagements, training programs, and discussions with executives in high-tech, industrial, and service industries.

Intrigued by this important professional challenge, market definition became my newfound passion. Furthermore, it was the perfect complement to my work in market segmentation. The timing was great. I was moving out of a career as a marketing practitioner and into my new profession as a marketing professor. My doctoral dissertation afforded me a wonderful opportunity to apply scholarship to a big, practical problem that ultimately determines the survival or failure of an organization (yes, relevance and rigor can peacefully coexist).

I have been researching, writing, and speaking about market definition in a business market context for more than eight years. I am truly convinced that understanding and exploiting markets must be the top priority for management. Market definition provides focus and direction for the organization; hence, this activity directly correlates with corporate performance. Unfortunately, caught up in the daily chaos of running complex organizations, many managers pay scant attention to market definition processes and strategies.

Defining Your Market is assembled from the latest thinking from the business and academic communities. It summarizes and extends my work and others' (leading marketing and management scholars) in this crucial area. Building on a dual foundation of conceptual and empirical study, the book provides a pragmatic and comprehensive knowledge base. It explores important marketing planning, research, and strategy issues affecting managers in changing and competitive industries (e.g., business products and services, health care, high-tech, industrial, professional services, etc.).

More important, *Defining Your Market* offers practical business ideas and field-tested solutions on how to effectively define and redefine markets. Insights and management implications are drawn from surveys, focus groups, and interaction with hundreds of marketing executives from dozens of excellent companies. Business practitioners can readily apply these valuable market planning tools. By learning how other companies in your industry or related industries define markets, you are able to adapt the "best practices" and incorporate them into strategy formation.

Defining Your Market was written to provide marketing practitioners, managers and executives, and scholars (professors and graduate students) with an informative, state-of-the-art guide to strategically defining business markets. Much of the material appearing in the book has been discussed at length in MBA and doctoral courses and in executive seminars. A Notes section appears at the end of the book and will direct readers to additional published works on topics of further interest. In addition to many useful corporate examples, figures, and tables, "Redefinition Remedies" (thought-provoking exercises) will help you put the concepts to immediate and profitable use.

Defining Your Market is organized into five parts. Part I, Defining Business Markets: A Primer (Chapters 1 and 2), examines the central role that market definition should take in an organization's strategic marketing planning function. The various approaches managers use to define markets, levels of market definition, avoiding marketing myopia, how to find relevant markets, and becoming market focused are discussed.

Part II, Market Definition: Research Findings (Chapter 3 through Chapter 7), presents issues and insights based on the market definition survey and related research initiatives. Market definition characteristics such as customer groups, customer functions, technologies, products, and competition; internal and external market definitions (customer and competitive market views); the market definition/segmentation link in business markets; market redefinition approaches and strategies; market definition criteria; and market conduct and performance relationships are some of the important ideas detailed.

Part III, Market Redefinition: Finding Strategic Advantage (Chapter 8 through Chapter 10), explains the major business implications of this market definition work. A three-stage framework for defining markets is introduced, strategic applications of market definition are reviewed, a seven-step market definition process is described, and lessons learned are revealed.

Part IV, Case Studies, offers hands-on examples of how to use this valuable material. The Newspaper Industry and Sportmed cases give readers a more in-depth look at how to define markets.

In Part V, Appendixes, the sample characteristics are summarized and the questionnaire used in the market definition survey is provided.

I believe that *visionary executives build markets today to become market leaders tommorrow!* I am pleased to offer you my blueprint for improving your business performance in new or existing markets. Enjoy the educational experience.

I look forward to learning more about your market definition trials, tribulations, and triumphs. Feel free to contact me at: 1-800-672-7223 ext. 5097, 954-262-3965 fax, or art@sbe.acast.nova.edu.

Art Weinstein, PhD
Professor of Marketing
Nova Southeastern University, SBE
Fort Lauderdale, Florida

Acknowledgments

Many individuals provided valuable input toward the preparation of *Defining Your Market*. First and foremost, I thank Bill Winston and the outstanding management team and staff at The Haworth Press for making this book possible. (Haworth knows how to define its market.)

Second, I thank my Nova Southeastern University colleagues. In particular, Bill Johnson and Herb Johnson each reviewed two chapters, offered helpful suggestions, and always demonstrated sound market judgment. Joanie Silverman, MBA, did a stellar job as my research assistant and located many of the important references used in the book. Isabell Layer's computer graphics work is consistently first-rate. Randy Pohlman, Dean of the School of Business and Entrepreneurship, has provided encouragement and the freedom to pursue a meaningful research agenda. And of course, my MBA and doctoral students provided a tremendous learning laboratory for reshaping this marketing message.

Third, I must acknowledge the following people for their critiques, illustrative examples, and insights at various stages of this project, from idea to finished product. In alphabetical order, thank you—Hilton Barrett, Frank Carmone, Alan S. Cleland, Jonathan Goodrich, Barnett Greenberg, Jim Haughey, Eugene J. Kelley, Gary Korenjel, George Matyjewicz, Marvin Nesbit, and Bruce Seaton. Also, my work was influenced by thinking espoused by Derek Abell, George Day, Gary Hamel, Philip Kotler, Ted Levitt, Allan Shocker, Jerry Wind, and other scholars.

Fourth, this book benefited substantially from "real world" business experiences gained over the years from thousands of marketing practitioners. Specifically, an expression of gratitude goes out to the 266 marketers who gave their valuable time and energy to participate in the qualitative and quantitative research phases. I also appreciate what I learned along the way about market definition from clients at Cordis/Johnson & Johnson, Hewlett-Packard, Intel, and Vacation Break; executive seminar participants at the University of Pittsburgh and Southern Methodist University; presentations to the California Newspaper Publishers Association, Society of Competitive Intelligence Professionals, and SoftEx 2000; and previous employers such as A.C. Nielsen, Pro-Mark Services, and the Small Business Development Center.

Last but not least, I especially thank you for reading *Defining Your Market*!

PART I:
DEFINING BUSINESS MARKETS:
A PRIMER

Chapter 1

Market Definition: An Overview

If you don't drive your business, you will be driven out of business.

— B. C. Forbes

Industries are not always well defined. Companies often invent new markets; sometimes knowingly, sometimes by accident.

—Vice President of Business Development, computer software firm

How do managers define the markets in which they compete? How should they define their markets? When should markets be redefined? Which redefinition strategies are most effective? These are some of the critical queries that successful marketers wrestle with on an ongoing basis. Customer needs, customer groups, technology, products, and competition play a pivotal role in the development of effective market definition strategies for business, service, and technology companies.

Merck, one of America's most admired companies, has prospered by understanding global health care markets. The company is not just a pharmaceuticals firm, but believes that it is in the health care management business. In fact, management states that its business is improving and preserving human life.[1]

In contrast, other once-successful companies can struggle with inadequate definitions of their markets. Case in point: Apple Computer. In 1995, Apple's Macintosh was cloned by Power Computing of Austin, Texas. It was six years too late. Apple's failure to license its technology allowed Microsoft's Mac-like Windows program to become the de facto industry standard in PC software.[2]

The Macintosh was well positioned as the computer for the non-technical masses (this is the same market that buys millions of those computer books for dummies and idiots, annually). Unfortunately, Apple's management team made a serious error in business judgment by stubbornly holding on to a narrow, proprietary technology. If Apple changed its market definition and opened its operating system software to the computer world, it is likely that the company would have posed a serious threat to Bill Gates and Microsoft.

DEFINING MARKETS:
THE STARTING POINT FOR STRATEGIC PLANNING

One of the most critical strategic decisions executives face is determining the optimal market definition for their company and business units. Company X may debate whether its business is copiers or automated office systems while Company Z might grapple with the idea of plastics or recyclable packaging materials. Newspaper publishers realize that they are no longer just in the news business. Their industry has been transformed from a print medium for large, general audiences to an information and entertainment services provider for smaller, highly-targeted audiences. Specialized advertisers must now appeal to segmented consumer markets (see Case Study 1, The U.S. Newspaper Industry, in Part IV of this book).

The restructuring of the health care market means that the traditional industry focus (medical treatment) has been supplanted by a newfound emphasis—wellness (i.e., health and prevention). Pharmaceutical companies are an integral part of this changing environment. Such companies as SmithKline Beecham (asthma), Novo Nordisk (diabetes), and Eli Lilly (cancer, cardiovascular, central nervous system, endocrine, and infectious conditions), are getting into the disease management business. Other firms are opting to become researcher-only specialists, development-only companies, wholesalers, or broadly defined health care providers to compete successfully in a volatile medical industry.[3]

Surprisingly, most firms pay scant attention to the focal business activity of market definition, which serves as the compass for navigating tough and turbulent competitive oceans. Few companies have established practical frameworks and knowledge systems to adequately define markets or, for that matter, designated individuals with the prime responsibility for monitoring and evaluating markets (market redefinition). This is particularly troubling since *market definition directly affects the overall success or failure of an organization.*

As a strategic mechanism that represents the heart of sound marketing and business planning, effective market definition assists management in a multiplicity of critical areas including:

- Formulating a business mission and vision
- Becoming more market/customer-oriented
- Developing competitive strategies
- Analyzing market share
- Expanding geographically or into new industry sectors
- Assessing merger/acquisition or divestiture options
- Evaluating potential market segments
- Devising appropriate positioning strategies
- Improving new product development initiatives
- Rethinking pricing, promotional, and distribution decisions

THE MARKET DEFINITION IMPERATIVE

The information superhighway offers excitement and promise to millions of American and worldwide users. Large companies and start-up firms are fighting aggressively to find their niche in this explosive marketplace. It is interesting to note that several major organizations (AT&T, Control Data, IBM, and the U.S. Postal Service) had a chance to establish leadership positions in the formative days of the Internet, yet they passed on these tremendous opportunities due to a lack of foresight.[4]

Market redefinition is a key issue for firms to better understand. A study of Canadian business indicated that a clear definition of what business(es) a company was in (and not in) and a clear understanding of the firm's critical success factors were the two areas identified as highest impact by senior executives.[5]

As its computer information market changed, CompuServe adapted from being a mainframe time-share service to a PC-based on-line service deliverer. A key part of its corporate evolution was the foray into full-service Internet access. However, as part of its corporate expansion strategy, CompuServe stretched its market definition too far. The company recently was forced to close its on-line, family-oriented service called WOW! to focus on what it does best—serving the business user.

Defining markets is a major problem for firms, large and small; as a result, it is a business activity often misunderstood or neglected by management. Given that this issue is so fundamental to marketing management, we would expect that market definition practices and theories would be systematically investigated, developed, and well-understood. However, research indicated that this clearly has not been the case.[6]

Recognize that markets are multidimensional—comprising people (present and potential customers), needs/wants, purchasing power, competitors, and environmental forces (e.g., technology, regulators, etc.)—as well as products. Rather than using an integrated approach, firms frequently define their markets solely via a product, an application, or a customer basis.

Market redefinition decisions are of considerable strategic and tactical consequence to the firm. The impact of effective or ineffective market definition is illustrated by the actions or inactions of eight leading companies during the past two decades (see Figure 1.1).

WHY MARKETS NEED TO BE REDEFINED

Cursory, intuitive, or informal market definitions are seldom effective in the fast-changing, highly competitive marketplace of the late 1990s, and the forthcoming new millennium. Hammer and Champy note that today's business environment is characterized by customers that take charge (buyer markets), competitive intensity (niche and global competitors that do not play by the rules), and constant change (product proliferation, ever-shortening product life cycles, and technological sophistication). To respond effectively, companies must move from task to process orientations.[7]

Management can prepare for the marketing challenges of the year 2000 (and beyond) by implementing a market redefinition initiative now. *Market redefinition requires a new strategic mind-set,*

FIGURE 1.1. The Pivotal Role of Market Redefinition

Company	Action/Inaction	Impact
American Express	Believing it was in the information and leisure business, the company tried to acquire McGraw-Hill and Disney.	These takeover candidates were incompatible with AMEX's core financial services business.
Apple Computers	Delayed market response.	Company missed initial explosive wave in portable and notebook computers. Rebounded from this slow start with the Powerbook.
General Electric	Top management stated that the company is in the business of creating businesses that are number one or two in their worldwide markets.	Major reorganization under the leadership of Jack Welch, CEO. GE has become a boundaryless company with an increased emphasis on high-tech, service, and global markets.
Hewlett-Packard	Transformation from a technology-driven to a marketing-driven company.	Redefined core businesses from being based on technologies to emphasizing customer needs (solutions).
Intel	Viewed the microprocessor as a niche product and initially omitted personal computers as a primary market for the 286 chip.	At first, company targeted automation, telecommunications, and vertical markets. Then, they jumped on the IBM PC bandwagon.
MCI	Redefined business from communications to information technologies.	Moved from a voice or data transportation source to a customer solution provider.
Polaroid	Myopic market definition.	Failed to commercialize new technologies developed in its laboratories.
Xerox	Third major shift in marketing philosophy—moved from being a copier company to an information company to "The Document Company."	Reorganization from functional lines to business units focusing on end customers.

organizational change in response to market forces, *reengineering of marketing processes* (e.g., marketing plans, marketing research approaches, segmentation analysis, implementation, and control), and *redesign of marketing programs* (target market selection and positioning, product development and management, pricing, promotion, and distribution).

Market redefinition is crucial (yet difficult to grasp) in many companies due to high levels of market and technological uncertainty. Hewlett-Packard (HP) successfully reinvented itself from a company driven by technology to one closely focused on the markets it serves. Today, HP's market orientation emphasizes customer solutions/needs relating to computing, communications, and measurement. And it is working in a big way. Benefiting primarily from printers, PCs, and large computer systems, this $38 billion revenue company (1996) is experiencing rapid growth in sales. Furthermore, it moves with small-firm agility into new markets. Products that have been introduced or revamped within the past two years now account for 70 percent of HP's orders, up from 30 percent a decade ago.[8]

Hewlett-Packard epitomizes the vital characteristics found in a company with the ability to "compete for the future." Hamel and Prahalad offer this insightful commentary:

> It is not enough for a company to get smaller and better and faster, as important as these tasks may be; a company must also be capable of fundamentally reconceiving itself, of regenerating its core strategies, and of reinventing its industry. In short, a company must also be capable of getting different.[9]

MARKET DEFINITION IS A PROCESS AND AN OUTCOME

What is really meant by the term *market definition?* Market definition has two meanings.[10] First, it refers to a summary statement of a business unit's core market strategy, with respect to customer needs, customer groups, technologies, etc. Here is an example of how a semiconductor company might define its market:

> We manufacture microprocessors, microcontrollers, computer boards, and related products serving the original equipment

manufacturers (OEM) computer market and related industries (industrial equipment, transportation, and medical equipment). Customers primarily in the Americas, Europe, and Asia will benefit from our cutting-edge technologies and outstanding service.

Second, there is the process by which companies define markets. This is the more important strategic issue to the firm. The summary statement logically flows from an effective market definition process. For some companies, market selection decisions are virtually nonexistent—top management dictates policy (e.g., our firm is in the direct mail advertising business) or no one in the organization consciously considers the relevance of the market definition issue. Without adaptation, these companies will not succeed in the long run in today's globally competitive markets.

Market-driven companies incorporate a strategic market definition process into their business planning initiatives (see Case Study 2, Sportmed, in Part IV of this book). Defining markets is not a one-shot effort, but rather requires periodic review and fine-tuning. A proactive stance toward understanding markets necessitates that a series of steps be implemented. A seven-step framework is advocated, as illustrated in Figure 1.2. This process is discussed further in Chapter 10. Redefinition Remedy 1, at the end of this chapter, gives you an opportunity to get a better handle on the nature of your business.

FIGURE 1.2. The Market Definition Process

1. Assess the impact of competition and market uncontrollables.
2. Instill a strong marketing and technological orientation within the firm.
3. Select the right mix of market definition characteristics.
4. Utilize market definition criteria.
5. Review and revise (if necessary) present market definitions.
6. Look to other companies/industries for market insight.
7. Implement and control new market definitions.

SUMMARY

Market definition plays a fundamental role in business/marketing strategy decisions. Although many executives feel that research and strategic planning are not essential (they believe that they "know" their business or they are more consumed with implementation issues/ fire fighting), such myopic thinking can yield catastrophic results. Drucker comments that while the question "what is our business?" often seems obvious, managerial neglect of this core doctrine is the number one cause of organizational frustration and failure. He adds that business definition should be built around customer needs and wants.[11]

This introductory chapter discussed four key market definition themes: (1) market definition as the starting point for strategic planning, (2) the market definition imperative for business, (3) why markets need to be redefined, and (4) market definition as a process and an outcome. The next chapter builds on these ideas and explains how market definition relates to market orientation and can be used to guide an organization's marketing planning, management, and strategic activities.

REDEFINITION REMEDY 1:
WHAT BUSINESS ARE YOU REALLY IN?

1. Management says that the purpose of our business is to: _____

_____

2. The top marketing executive in our company says we are in business to: _____

_____

3. Your customers' primary needs are:_____

_____

4. What key benefits are customers seeking? _____

_____

5. What new technologies are customers seeking? _____

_____

6. Which market segments are you targeting? _____

_____

7. What products should you be providing to your customers that you are not currently offering? Why aren't these available?__

_____

8. What is your competitive advantage?_____

_____

9. In ten words or less, describe the nature of your business today:_____

In two years: _____

In five years: _____

Management Challenge

• Based on your brief responses to the above questions, what strategic changes does your company need to make today to be more competitive tomorrow? How should you redefine markets?

Chapter 2

Defining Markets: Key Concepts

Changing the direction of a large company is like trying to turn an aircraft carrier. It takes a mile before anything happens. And if it was a wrong turn, getting back on course takes even longer.

—Al Ries and Jack Trout

We can define the market in many ways. We now are in the process of moving to much wider markets.

—President, electronics company

Market definition provides the basis for effective marketing and business strategy. Organizations must become market driven to compete effectively in changing and competitive markets. In this chapter, we will learn how to create a market-oriented culture. First, the previous research on market definition will be highlighted. Second, the idea of levels of market definition—corporate, business, and program—will be introduced. Third, the relevant market concept will be explained. This chapter concludes with an extended discussion on what it really means to be market focused (i.e., market orientation insights, realistic applications for mission and vision statements, and market/customer ownership guidelines).

MARKET DEFINITION: CONTRIBUTIONS TO THE LITERATURE

An introductory review of market definition was developed by Jack Sissors more than thirty years ago. In his *Journal of Marketing* article titled "What Is a Market?," he identified eight ways that prospects for a product market could be defined.[1] These included: (1) size of the market, (2) geographic location of purchasers, (3) demographics, (4) social-psychological characteristics, (5) reasons why products are purchased, (6) who makes/influences decisions, (7) when purchases are made, and (8) how purchasing is done (e.g., impulse versus brand request, quantity/frequency of units purchased, etc.). While little new information is presented in his model and these eight approaches may be better characterized as consumer segmentation dimensions than market descriptors, the value of Sissors' work lies in his explanation that markets should be studied as a conceptual whole (the Gestalt approach) rather than fragmentary parts.

Market structurists have attempted to clarify the interrelationship of firms, products, and potential customers. One camp of scholars defined markets through models and frameworks. Myers and Tauber's conceptual models progressed from a supply-side economics perspective (i.e., evaluating the number and types of firms in an industry) to comprehensive demand-side market frameworks that consider customer characteristics and behaviors.[2]

Russ Haley views markets as a series of concentric competitive rings.[3] The innermost ring is the firm's most immediate competition, while the outermost rings are indirect competitors. Although interesting, this approach does not provide a mechanism for deciding at what level (ring) the company should compete. This decision is the determination of your relevant market, which is discussed later in this chapter.

A second group of market structurists, spearheaded by Bourgeois, Day, Shocker, and Srivastava, used hierarchical clustering and multidimensional scaling techniques to define product markets.[4] This work provided some insight on identifying product-market boundaries, product substitutability, segmentation, and strategic marketing via usage behavior and judgmental approaches (e.g., customer judgments, perceptual mapping, and protocol analysis) in various market situations.

Excluding my work, which is summarized in this book, empirical research on industrial market definition is surprisingly limited. Frazier and Howell analyzed strategic groups of wholesalers in the medical supply and equipment channel.[5] They assessed various financial, strategic, and operational variables. The Profit Impact of Market Strategies

(PIMS) program provides a wealth of of financial and marketing data, some quite useful to firms in understanding business markets.[6]

Perhaps the most important contribution to the market definition literature was provided by Derek Abell.[7] His multidimensional approach states that markets are principally composed of customer groups (market segments), customer functions and uses (market needs), and technology and materials. He adds that geography, level of production and distribution, and environmental factors may also be considered in certain market situations. Abell's work is quite significant; in fact, it provides the basis for the research conducted and reported in Chapter 3 (market definition characteristics) and Chapter 6 (market redefinition).

THREE LEVELS OF MARKET DEFINITION

Business definition is the first step toward sound strategic marketing planning. Nevertheless, markets are often defined by accident rather than design. Abell remarks that market definition can take place at three levels within the firm: (1) corporate, (2) business, and (3) program.[8]

The corporate level, the strategic management perspective, is responsible for determining the firm's business mission. At the top level, a vision for the organization is articulated by senior management.

Historically, accounting firms provided auditing and tax preparation services for their clients. Facing squeezed profit margins in these core businesses and new competition from law firms (e.g., tax attorneys), certified financial planners (CFPs), and a variety of financial consultants, senior partners are reexamining the very essence of their profession. Some CPA firms say that if you can't beat them, you might as well join them; they are hiring CFPs, tax litigators, and tax planners and are evolving into financial services firms.

Others are forming strategic alliances within or outside their fields. In an attempt to replicate H & R Block's remarkable success as a Sears "partner" (1993 revenues of over $1 billion from more than 700 North American Sears sites), Jackson Hewitt, which already has a presence in 200 Montgomery Ward stores, is linking up with Wal-Mart superstores.[9]

Arthur Andersen and Company's spin-off of its consulting arm (Andersen Consulting) created two well-focused enterprises poised to respond to today's accounting and management advisory challenges. Andersen Worldwide now generates more than half of its revenues from its consulting business. Some industry observers recommend that the consulting operation should again split into computer and management services to sustain its double-digit growth patterns. Over a five-year-period ending in 1995, consulting revenues have grown from 14 to 22 percent of the total business at the 100 largest U.S. accounting firms (the numbers were 27 and 34 percent, respectively, for the Big 6 firms).[10]

Product and market strategy are formulated at the business level (e.g., strategic business unit or SBU). Small and medium-sized accounting firms (as well as the Big 6) are venturing into nontraditional areas to boost their bottom lines. To diversify and stay ahead of the pack, CPA firms are introducing a battery of new services such as computerized accounting and information systems, international business expansion services (e.g., market entry advisement, country/ location analysis, foreign tax advice, etc.), management training, feasibility studies, financial planning, etc. Such profit centers help to offset millions of dollars in lost revenues from tax software packages such as TurboTax.

Segmentation and positioning decisions are executed at the program level. Many companies are opting to specialize by industry (e.g., health care, sports management, tourism, etc.). In addition to tax preparation, Jackson Hewitt is now providing pack-and-mail services to mitigate the inherent seasonality of their business.

While all three market definition levels (corporate, business, and program) are vital, interconnected, and will be explored further, *the "presegmented" market (level 2), is the primary focus of this book.* Figure 2.1 summarizes the organizational unit, management responsibility, and strategic thrust for the market definition levels.

AVOIDING MARKETING MYOPIA: FINDING YOUR RELEVANT MARKET

Ted Levitt's insightful commentary on myopic market definitions by the railroads, the Hollywood movie industry, and buggy whip

FIGURE 2.1. Levels of Market Definition

Organizational Unit	Management Level Responsibility	Strategic Thrust
1. Corporate	Top management	Business mission
2. Business (SBU)	Middle-upper level marketing management	Product/market strategy
3. Program	Lower-middle level marketing management	Segmentation/ positioning

manufacturers has been preached to hundreds of thousands of MBAs in marketing management courses. This message is nearly forty-years-old, but it is by no means dated. If you have not read "Marketing Myopia," read it; if you have read it, think about reading it again![11]

Levitt warned practitioners to reexamine their markets and take a customer orientation rather than a product focus. Executives can clearly benefit by defining their business as transportation or business knowledge/intelligence rather than railroading or market research. As an example, a buyer of marketing information notes that the market research industry seldom practices what it preaches to clients. Firms often produce reams of data on attitudes, habits, and so on (a focus on the techniques) without explicitly considering how this research can be used to develop business strategies (solve problems).[12]

According to Richard, Womack, and Allaway, organizations may exhibit various forms of marketing myopia.[13] The classic myopic firm has a product definition and a single-industry perspective (for example, an advertising agency that targets automobile dealers and specializes in broadcast media). The competitive myopic firm has a customer definition and a single-industry perspective (the ad agency that provides a complete line of tailored corporate communications and promotional services). The efficiency myopic firm utilizes a product definition with a multi-industry perspective (the ad agency limits its work to television and radio commercials but offers its services to a wider range of clients in banking, health care, retail, and service sectors).

To avoid marketing myopia, a desired state is the innovative firm that employs a customer definition and a multi-industry perspective.

In this case, the advertising agency continues to serve various markets but evolves into a marketing consulting firm and offers (directly or through subcontracting arrangements) strategic planning advice, marketing research studies, integrated marketing communications programs, or other marketing services dictated by client needs.

Market expansion is a sound business strategy, but companies should carefully evaluate how far they stretch and in what directions. Has Richard Branson's Virgin (UK) conglomerate gone too far with respect to its diverse business interests? While his Virgin Records Megastores is a formidable competitor to Blockbuster, Tower, Sam Goody, and others in the music business, and has a relatively strong niche in the airline industry competing head-to-head with British Airways, how successful will Virgin Cola be competing with Coca-Cola in the global soft drink marketplace? Determining your *relevant market—the market appropriate for your firm given its objectives, resources, and environment*—is a prerequisite for success in fast-changing and highly competitive industries. Defining markets too narrowly limits business opportunities; it instills a production-driven corporate culture, rather than a true market-based view. Looking to the night sky for insight, an astronomical analogy can tell us whether your company is Ptolemaic (earth/products at the center of its universe) or Copernican (sun/customers at the center of its universe) in its marketing thinking.

Take the case of a single-product entrepreneurial company that has developed an easy to use, yet powerful desktop faxing software. This computer program images documents on-screen, enabling users to send mass faxes to multiple recipients. Prior to implementing expansion plans, this firm needs to carefully evaluate its relevant market (computerized business communication) to find new market opportunities. The newer technologies such as electronic and voice mail, manual facsimile machines, on-line services and the Internet, plus the mainstream offerings such as telephone, mail, and overnight services, and emerging technologies should all be contemplated in moving this small business beyond its product market.

A market definition too broad is equally dangerous. It can lead to a mass marketing mentality and overlook profitable niches in the marketplace. If this company tries to be in the *general communication* business (generic market) rather than the *computerized business communication* business (relevant market) it will clearly be over-matched by telecommunications providers such as AT&T, MCI, Sprint, the regional Bells, and dozens of other local service providers and manufacturers of mainstream facsimile machines (e.g., Brother, Sharp, Xerox, etc.).

The relevant market is much larger than the product market; in fact, it may include many related product markets. It is also much smaller and more focused than the generic market (see Figure 2.2). The shaded area indicates that the relevant markets are dynamic and should be monitored and evaluated on an ongoing basis.

The "right" relevant market allows companies to compete successfully by focusing on what they do best, whether it is operational excellence, product leadership, or customer intimacy.[14] Operationally excellent companies such as Dell Computer provide customers with readily available, reliable products at competitive prices. Product leaders such as Johnson & Johnson stress innovation and build

FIGURE 2.2. Finding the Relevant Market—An Example

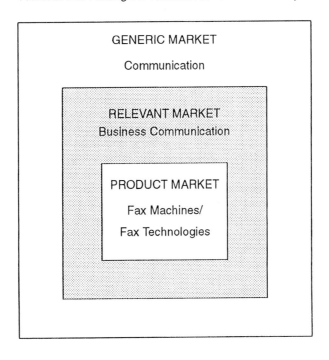

offerings that outperform the competition. Customer-intimate firms such as Airborne Express understand and respond quickly to customer needs.

Once a market definition has been accepted by marketing management, it serves as the foundation upon which the marketing mix can be formulated and implemented. The concept of levels of market definition (corporate, business unit, and program) means that STP marketing—segmentation, targeting, and positioning—can only be successfully developed and implemented once a definition of the "presegmented" market has been determined.

Let's revisit the semiconductor company's market definition (introduced in Chapter 1). "The manufacturing of microprocessors, microcontrollers, computer boards, and related products" is the *product market* definition. Extending this product focus to the global computer industry and other industry sectors utilizing computer components is a *generic market* definition. Its *relevant market* might be defined as leading-edge, original equipment manufacturers (OEMs) growing 5 percent or more annually.

With this operating market definition in place, management can then segment its two core markets: computer and noncomputer, to find attractive niche opportunities. While the former presents numerous, readily apparent avenues to explore such as relationships with companies producing desktops, portables, multimedia, and communications technology, the latter may offer less obvious but highly profitable segments. These include, but are by no means limited to, the automotive and transportation market, the oil industry, industrial process controls, medical technology, and a plethora of other options requiring further market analysis.

HOW TO BECOME MARKET FOCUSED

Organizations that build on a clear, concise, and consistent business philosophy (based on an effective market definition basis) are capable of winning/dominating their markets. Managerial focus is the roadmap providing strategic direction to the firm. Since companies have unique strengths and core competencies, they will excel in different areas. Companies should carefully evaluate their greatest strength; this strategic thrust can be used as a basis for designing overall business strategy.

For example, in the car rental business four factors are widely acknowledged as being critical success factors in the industry: good service, good value, product availability, and on-airport location. A firm that offers exceptional service (which includes express check-in and checkout) or hourly rentals can use their singular key advantage as a business thrust.

A business thrust might be based on marketing or nonmarketing factors (e.g., management expertise, research and development capabilities, manufacturing or operations strengths, etc.). In the latter case, it is marketing's challenge to successfully communicate this core competence to its target markets. An example of some highly respected business, service, and technology companies and their strategic thrusts are listed in Table 2.1.

TABLE 2.1. Examples of Corporate Strategic Thrusts

Company	Strategic Thrust
General Electric	Overall Marketing Expertise
Hewlett-Packard	Segmentation/Target Marketing
Motorola	Product/Service
Quick & Reilly	Pricing
Cordis Corporation/ Johnson & Johnson	Sales/Promotion
Dell Computer	Distribution
Ryder System	Logistics
Intel	Innovation
Emerson Electric	Manufacturing
Fedex	Operations
American Express	Finance
Dun & Bradstreet	Business Information

Market Orientation

Market orientation is the firm's implementation of the marketing concept. The marketing concept is a guiding business doctrine advocating a company-wide effort to satisfy both customers and organizational objectives (in particular, profitability). A market-oriented organization is one whose actions are consistent with the marketing concept. Market-oriented organizations are customer focused while production-oriented firms stress a product focus. In addition to implementing the marketing concept, marketing-oriented firms utilize marketing activities prior to developing a marketing mix/strategy. These activities include market definition as well as segmentation/ target market selection, marketing research, sales forecasting, etc.

While consumer-oriented companies such as General Electric, Nordstrom's, Procter & Gamble, Sony, Toyota, and others have employed marketing-oriented thinking for several decades, this business philosophy is a relatively newer phenomenon for many of the companies featured in this book. On the plus side, great progress already has been made; business-to-business and high-tech companies, as well as health care organizations (such as hospitals, HMOs, and medical practices), and professional service providers (attorneys, CPA firms, management consultants, etc.), have embraced marketing in recent years.

Regardless of the type of company you may work for, a market orientation provides the impetus for building an organizational culture that puts the customer first, creates superior value for your customers, and leads to increased overall business performance. Employees of market-oriented companies become value providers; they know the importance of listening to and responding to customers. DuPont's "Adopt a Customer" program is one example of a successful customer-focused initiative. Workers visit customers monthly, learn their needs, and are their representatives on the factory floor.[15]

Recognize that today's customers are quite sophisticated. They are choice-seeking, demanding, knowledgeable, less loyal, price conscious, time impoverished, and value-seeking. Personalized marketing relationships must be built through databases/marketing information systems, research, integrated marketing communications (IMC), and the human touch (getting close to customers) to ensure customer retention.

Astute marketers go beyond satisfying customers: they are able to predict customer needs and wants and practice anticipatory marketing. According to Barrett, there is a five-stage bias for action continuum.[16]

At the nonresponsive level, there is limited awareness of external stimuli (e.g., IBM initially ignored the PC market). At the reactive level, the firm is aware of the stimuli, but only after repeated prodding does it react (e.g., Xerox was slow in developing competitive strategies to win back the low-end sector of the copier market from Canon in the 1980s).

Most companies are at the responsive level. Customers may force the firm to enter new product markets, sometimes reluctantly. Many companies will then take appropriate action, assuming the opportunity fits the present business mission and adequate resources are available.

Proactiveness is the fourth stage and implies corporate entrepreneurship has surfaced in the organization. This means that larger companies simulate the innovation, flexibility, creativity, and speed to market of their smaller counterparts.

Anticipatory marketing is the aspirational level, attained by relatively few firms (and then only infrequently). At this point, companies understand virtually all of the market nuances and treat their customers as business allies and partners. Kinko's Copy Centers have done a good job in this area by offering round-the-clock service and anticipating the desires of its customer base in its new product offerings. A strong market orientation and effective market definition can guide organizations through the continuum to, ultimately, the proactive and anticipatory stages.

Market orientation became a trendy research priority in the 1990s.[17] Managers know that becoming market oriented favorably affects business performance. Yet, there are relatively few studies of the consequences of a market orientation. According to Narver and Slater, market orientation consists of three behavioral components—customer orientation, competitor orientation, and interfunctional coordination—and two decision criteria, long-term focus and profitability. While their research supported the former set, the latter issues (although intuitively logical) were not empirically validated. Kohli and Jaworski add that the market orientation construct comprises intelligence generation, intelligence dissemination, and responsiveness. Hence, a true market orientation must balance customer and competitive factors.

Firms operating in competitive industries are most likely to benefit from a market orientation. In a five-state study of 293 hospital executives from 176 institutions, Raju, Lonial, and Gupta found that "responsiveness to competition" was the only aspect of market orientation that correlated with all three hospital performance dimensions tested—financial performance, market/product development, and internal quality.[18]

Since competitive markets provide more product offerings to customers, it is necessary for firms to be more "in touch" with their markets. Practicing the marketing concept, using market research, sales forecasting, and target marketing—adopting a marketing orientation—is an effective strategic response to competitive pressures. Market orientation inputs are valuable for formulating an initial market definition and are provided in Redefinition Remedy 2.

Mission, Vision, and Market Definition

Market-focused companies integrate market definitions into corporate and business unit planning frameworks to guide programs, processes, products, and people. Market definition provides a springboard for the development of mission and vision statements that work rather than just look good on paper.

Business performance demonstrates that mission statements are effective. A 1994 study of *Business Week* 1,000 companies showed that companies that had mission statements reported an average return on stockholder equity of 16.1 percent versus 9.7 percent for those that lacked this strategic planning document.[19]

Based on the literature, effective mission statements must be clearly articulated, relevant, current, written in a positive (inspiring tone), unique to the organization, enduring, and adapted to the target audience.[20] Furthermore, mission statements should be brief but complete, provide strategic direction, present the big picture, lead to results, and help answer such basic questions as:

- What business are we really in?
- How is our business changing?

- What other businesses do we need to be in?
- Who are our customers?
- What do our customers want?
- How do we create, maximize, and deliver value to our customers?
- What is our business philosophy?
- How are we different (and better) than our competitors?

Health care organizations should incorporate key ideas from their constituencies to provide input for developing mission statements. These prime parties include patients, physicians, payors, and people (the community). Johnson & Johnson's credo is that their first responsibility is to customers (doctors, nurses, patients, and all users of their products and services), their second responsibility is to their employees, their third responsibility is to their local and world communities, and their final responsibility is to their stockholders.[21]

While the mission states what your business is today, the vision statement is future-directed and should revitalize the organization; it looks at your business tommorrow—five-to-ten-year views typically work well, although many Japanese companies use a much longer planning horizon. A vision may represent an ideal scenario, but it is doable if the organization's people perform to their capabilities. BellSouth's vision is to be the customer's best connection to communications, information, and entertainment.

According to Collins and Porras, a well-conceived vision consists of a core ideology and an envisioned future.[22] The former typically comprises three to five central values and the establishment of a guiding long-term purpose. The latter identifies bold, stretch goals (called big, hairy, audacious goals or BHAGS) and exploits the organization's core competences.

While vision statements can be a highly valuable market planning tool, research shows that there are relatively few truly visionary leaders. One study reported that only 5 percent of companies had strong vision statements and less than 1 percent had ones that were effectively communicated to their people.[23] Vision statements sometimes fail because they are viewed as fads. Hamermesh stated that in the early 1990s, as the company was losing $5 billion, Digital Equipment Corporation never saw a buzzword or hot new idea that they did not like. Taken to an extreme, a Dilbert-like management culture dominates. Consider this amusing quotation:

> Please develop a vision and be empowered and take a risk— and work in teams while you're doing it. And don't forget to manage by objective. And please get on with the quality movement. Oh, and by the way, manage with the fifth discipline and get close to your customers.[24]

Strong companies do not fall into the "searching for the magical answer" trap. Cemer is a Kansas City, Missouri-based, medium-sized company that creates clinical information systems designed to automate the patient care process for diagnosing and treating medical problems. Their straight, to-the-point mission—to automate the process of health care—is nicely complemented by an expanded vision statement (see Figure 2.3).[25]

FIGURE 2.3. Cemer's Vision

Cemer believes that all clinical information within a community should interrelate to create the foundation for high-quality, efficient health care. Cemer's vision is that our patient-focused system will empower health care enterprises to establish this foundation. Our vision is embodied in Cemer's Healthcare Network Architecture (HNA). HNA is not a product but a benefit of combining Cemer's products and other clinical information technologies. HNA enables health care enterprises to achieve benefits greater than the sum of their investments in clinical information technology.

Source: Abrahams, Jeffrey. *The Mission Statement Book,* (Ten Speed Press, 1995, pp. 162-163).

Own Your Markets and Customers

Ideally, companies should aspire to *market and customer ownership.* Since effective market definitions are unique, antitrust concerns are not necessarily a threat. Market ownership implies the identification of *distinctive business opportunities* (DBOs).

The implication is that it is better to control a majority of a well-defined market sector (be the big fish in the small pond) than to have a small share of a broad market (be a small fish in a giant lake). In the former case, customers will place your organization at the head of their mental list as the company that can best satisfy their needs. This high degree of awareness is unlikely to exist in the latter case.

According to Sherden, firms should be able to assess six key factors—customer segment, product/service, needs and values, channel, functions, and geography—in defining distinct businesses.[26] Two health care examples of the DBO concept include an HMO's annual prepaid family program and a one-stop, holistically-based medical clinic targeting senior citizens.

The capability of owning customers, whether existing, emerging, or even imagined, is the key to acheiving a sustainable competitive advantage. Companies such as Citibank, Fedex, Rank Xerox, and Zurich Insurance have embraced this strategy. Vandermerwe said it best:

> "Owning" customers means being the first choice for individuals who want you as a lifelong partner because you represent a long-term value to them in the same way that they do to you—and individual customers need offerings to suit their unique and changing needs over time.[27]

SUMMARY

Sound marketing/business strategy is closely linked to the market-based strategic planning approaches that firms use. Defining markets is at the heart of this process. In this chapter, the basic market-driven issues were explored to provide a conceptual framework for management. In particular, we examined previous important work on defining markets; corporate, business, and program levels of market definition; how to overcome myopic, product-oriented thinking by identifying appropriate, relevant markets; what it means to be market focused; the need for implementing a market orientation in an organization; how to benefit from mission and vision statements; and why owning markets and customers should be a prime business objective. In the next chapter, we will investigate how customer groups, customer needs, technologies, products, and competition are used to define markets.

REDEFINITION REMEDY 2:
THE INITIAL MARKET DEFINITION

Market definition begins with management commitment and market focus. After reviewing your responses to the questions describing "What Business Are You Really In?" (Redefinition Remedy 1), consider the following market-driven queries in your strategic marketing planning process.

1. Does your organization stress operational excellence, product leadership, or customer intimacy? _____

2. What is your guiding strategic thrust? _____

3. Do you have brief but substantive mission and vision statements? _____ (*Review these documents carefully and modify as necessary, or make the preparation of these materials a major priority over the next thirty days.*)

4. How market oriented is your organization? Explicitly consider the following attributes:
   a. customer orientation _____
   b. competitive orientation _____
   c. interfunctional coordination _____
   d. market-driven objectives _____
   e. market performance measures _____
   f. market intelligence utilization _____
   g. target marketing _____

5. How is value created, delivered, monitored, and maximized in your organization?

Management Challenge

- Identify your current product markets and generic markets.
- Based on this determination, preliminarily describe the "right" relevant markets for your organization.

PART II:
MARKET DEFINITION:
RESEARCH FINDINGS

Chapter 3

Five Critical
Market Definition Dimensions

The secret of business is to know something that nobody else does.

—Aristotle Onassis

Technology and markets change daily; what may have been a viable solution for a particular customer may not be the same solution for another customer in essentially the same business.

—President, computer hardware company

Executives realize that market/business definition is an essential strategic decision in today's volatile and globally competitive markets. Business, service, and technology firms can define markets in many different ways. The use of some approaches may result in highly effective market definitions, while other techniques are relatively unsuccessful. A solid market definition provides a sound conceptual framework for formulating management strategy. Building on research findings, this chapter provides managers with the working tools needed to formulate an initial or improved market definition.

THE 3-D MODEL: CUSTOMER GROUPS, CUSTOMER FUNCTIONS, AND TECHNOLOGIES

An important multidimensional view of market definition consists of customer groups (market segments), customer functions and uses (market needs), and technologies. This model, developed by Abell[1] and advocated by Buzzell,[2] is called 3-D analysis—selecting an appropriate three-dimensional "cell" defines the firm's market. In Abell's more current work, he argues that new technologies generate new product forms; hence, he now calls the technology dimension product/service forms.[3] Although Abell and Buzzell acknowledge that markets may have more than three critical dimensions (e.g., they also cited geography and level of production and distribution as possibilities), they limit their analysis to those key factors that can be visually represented.

An in-depth view of the PC sector using this approach is depicted in Figure 3.1. As the graphic illustrates, management has chosen to

FIGURE 3.1. A Market Definition Map of the PC Sector

CUSTOMER NEEDS
|
Multimedia
|
Wireless
Communication
|
Laptop *
|
Notebook
|
Handheld
|

TECHNOLOGIES | CUSTOMER GROUPS

386 | Education
486 SL/SX | Small Office/Home Office
486 DX | Scientists/Engineers
*** **Pentium** | **Business Travelers ***
Pentium Pro | Vertical/Niche Markets
Pentium MMX | International Markets
Pentium II/MMX | Government

*** Market definition selected

serve a market consisting of business travelers (customer group), laptops (customer need for powerful hardware), and Pentium chip products (technology). Note that this initial market definition is only one of many possible combinations that could be pursued by the company. As the organization grows, it can then evaluate dozens of alternative redefinitions and select the best options given the constraints of its capabilities, competitive situation, objectives, and resources.

Northern Valve, Inc. provides a second example of 3-D analysis in action. This company is small but successful in the highly fragmented industrial valve market. As Table 3.1 shows, Northern Valve has strategically broadened its market scope (with respect to all three core market definition determinants) to take advantage of new business opportunities. This new market definition allows the firm to position the product as one that could be used at different points in the production value chain (previously, the company focused exclusively on the pollution control sector in manufacturing plants). Hence, new products

TABLE 3.1. Two 3-D Views of Northern Valve's Market

Dimensions	Market Definition—Original	Market Definition–Emerging
Customer Functions	Collecting and discharging materials, airlock sealing	Collecting and discharging materials, airlock sealing, material flow control (gates)
Customer Segments	Mining, cement	Mining, cement, powder and bulk solids processing, energy and power, chemicals
Technology	Durable alloy casting and machining, pivoting dust valve	Durable alloy casting and machining, pivoting valve (various), gate valves

Source: McTavish, Ron. "One More Time: What Business Are You In?" *Long-Range Planning,* 28(2), 1995, pp. 49-60.

were introduced since customer plants were now envisioned as total flow process systems rather than just sites for dust valve applications.[4]

MARKET SCOPE: BROAD OR NARROW?

Realize that the decision to revisit market scope can result in one of three possible scenarios for each of the three core dimensions (needs, groups, and technologies) and the aggregate market definition: (1) a broadened market definition, (2) a narrower market definition, or (3) no change.

If in doubt, the firm might begin with a reasonable, but relatively narrow market definition (the highest level of disaggregation). As the transportation market illustrates, Justice Department merger guidelines suggest that this could be the safest strategy to pursue.[5] In one longitudinal study of semisubmersible rigs for offshore oil drilling, a national market definition was deemed best (subnational, regional, and global views were also considered). Market definition is important because it affects the set of competitive entrants, market boundaries, and performance measures.[6]

As a company grows and better understands its business, customers, competitors, and environmental forces, the market can then be widened, as appropriate. The "broadest market" approach was found to accurately reflect the competitive and regulatory concerns evidenced in many complex, technology-driven markets. The Taligent (IBM-Apple) joint venture received Federal Trade Commission (FTC) approval based on this test. The FTC realized that this new software venture would have minimal impact on overall market concentration, given all of the substitutes and sectors in the computer industry.[7]

Since antitrust enforcement is often based on analyses of market definition and market share, a "rule of reason" is often the chosen compromise position. The Herfindahl-Hirschman Index (HHI) is a tool frequently used to assess market concentration levels. HHI is defined as the sum of the squares of the market shares of all firms in the market. In merger cases, markets (postmerger) with HHIs of under 1,000 are seldom enforced; 1,000 to 1,800 may be enforced; and those exceeding 1,800 are very likely to be enforced.[8]

IMPORTANCE/SUCCESS EVALUATION
OF MARKET DEFINITION CHARACTERISTICS

Although 3-D analysis represents a valuable starting point for defining markets, this approach may be viewed as simplistic. Hence, a more comprehensive view of market definition is desirable. To assess how effectively the 3-D approach works and possible refinements in such methodology, an empirical test was conducted. The three critical dimensions—*customer groups, customer functions,* and *technologies,* and five others—*competition, environmental factors* (i.e., economic, political, and regulatory), *geographical area, market share,* and *products* were presented to marketing executives in a research study.[9] The sample profile of these marketers is provided in Appendix A (Part V of this book).

The importance of the market definition characteristics and managers' success in understanding and evaluating each factor was assessed. Hence, our first two research questions (RQ) investigated are listed in Figure 3.2.

FIGURE 3.2. Market Definition Characteristics—Research Questions

- **RQ1:** Which factors are most important to marketing managers in defining markets?
- **RQ2:** How successful are they in utilizing the market definition characteristics?

Measurement and Analytical Approach

A constant-sum scale was developed for the eight market definition characteristics tested in RQ1: competition, customer groups, customer functions, environmental factors, geographic area, market share, products, and technologies. Respondents could allocate a total of 100 points to as many or as few characteristics as they wished based on their perceived importance. Using the same eight factors, five-point (1 = unsuccessful to 5 = very successful) market definition success indicators were then obtained from respondents. Market definition success (a business perfomance dimension) is conceptualized as being able to understand and evaluate markets. The full survey is reproduced in Appendix B (Part V of this book).

Importance-performance analysis is a graphical technique for measuring attributes relevant in business strategy decisions.[10] This approach was recently used to assess the inpatient and outpatient medical services market for a midwestern, private hospital.[11]

Mean metric coordinates of the eight market definition characteristics can be plotted in two-dimensional space. The results of this four-quadrant analysis indicates market definition determinants:

Quadrant I.	Important and the firm is able to understand and evaluate
Quadrant II.	Important but the firm is *not* able to understand and evaluate
Quadrant III.	*Unimportant* but the firm is able to understand and evaluate
Quadrant IV.	*Unimportant* and the firm is *unable* to evaluate

This grid-based analysis provides important insights for marketers on areas worthy of concentration (Quadrant I), opportunities for improvement (Quadrant II), and areas that are relatively unimportant for market definition (Quadrants III and IV).

Findings

As revealed in Figure 3.3, business executives place different priorities on the characteristics used for defining markets.[12] Of the eight attributes tested via the 100-point constant-sum scale, five clearly emerged as important. Customer needs (31.5) was nearly twice as important as any other factor. Dr. Allen Meisel, Vice President for Customer Advocacy for Pfizer, Inc. explains the importance of putting customers first:

> Pharmaceutical companies have essentially ignored their customers in the past. We saw ourselves as suppliers of a technically unique product and that's all we did. One of the shifts that's going on in the pharmaceutical industry is that we're becoming

FIGURE 3.3. Market Definition Characteristics—An Importance/Success (I/S) Analysis

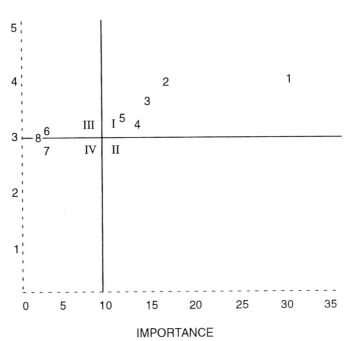

SUCCESS

IMPORTANCE

Legend:

Variables	I/S Rating
1. Customer needs	31.5, 3.8
2. Technology	16.5, 3.8
3. Competition	14.9, 3.6
4. Customer groups	14.6, 3.5
5. Products	12.0, 3.7
6. Geographic area	3.5, 3.2
7. Environmental factors	3.5, 2.8
8. Market share	3.3, 3.0

more customer focused. And part of the customer focus is not only listening to the customer, but incorporating that information back into the company and adjusting your behavior.[13]

Burton-Marstellar, a public relations powerhouse (sixty-three offices in thirty-eight countries) has emulated the business model of major consulting firms and no longer groups clients by geography. Their new approach stresses customer needs in ten practice areas—advertising, corporate, creative services, government, health care, marketing, media and community relations, perception management consulting, public affairs, and technology.[14]

A second set of factors—technology (16.5), competition (14.9), customer groups (14.6), and products (12.0)—yielded fairly similar mean importance scores. Three other characteristics—environmental factors, geographic area, and market share—were rated as relatively unimportant to business, service, and technology marketers with mean scores of 3.5, 3.5, and 3.3, respectively.

As Figure 3.4 depicts, the 3-D model is conceptually sound, but it does not account for 37 percent of managers' market definitions. Adding products and competition to the three established factors (customer needs, customer groups, and technologies) results in an improved 90 percent accountability for the new model. Although this revision is called the 5-D model (Figure 3.5), one might argue that

FIGURE 3.4. Market Definition—The 3-D Model

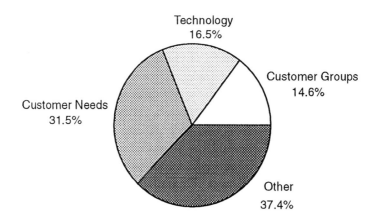

it is really a 1 + 4 model with one critical factor, customer needs, and four other important factors: customer groups, technologies, competition, and products (these latter elements are fairly similar in weighting, representing 12 to 16.5 percent of the market definition).

FIGURE 3.5. Market Definition—The 5-D Model

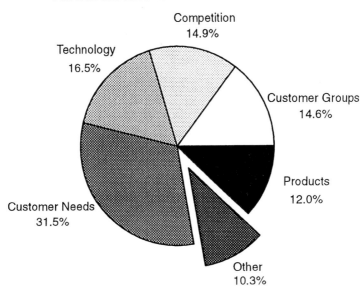

THE REVISED 5-D MODEL:
THE 3-Ds PLUS PRODUCTS AND COMPETITION

The research findings regarding market definition characteristics provide an important extension to Abell's 3-D model of market definition. Customer needs (functions), technology, and customer groups were ranked first, second, and fourth, respectively. Hence, we can say that Abell's theory was reasonably on-target. Based on the empirical investigation, however, competition and products should be added to a revised 5-D model. In fact, only 24 percent of the respondents used three or fewer dimensions to define markets. Two measures of central tendency for the number of market definition characteristics used (mean = 4.6 and median = 5.0) support the more comprehensive 5-D framework.

As the Importance-Success grid in Figure 3.3 depicts, business marketers also rated the five important dimensions relatively high in success (Quadrant I). In contrast, with respect to the less important factors, managers could successfully understand and evaluate geographic area (Quadrant III) but not market share or environmental factors (Quadrant IV). Based on this graphical analysis, marketing managers have done a good job in prioritizing key attributes of market definition. Their strengths are in relatively important areas and weaknesses in unimportant areas. Additionally, there are no characteristics located in the important/less successful space (Quadrant II). Such positioning would require immediate management attention.

The increased global scope of corporations suggests the need for a richer understanding of *customer needs. Technology, competition, customer groups*, and *products* (the other components of the 5-D market definition) must also be carefully analyzed by companies to develop winning strategies for the global marketplace. Case in point: BellSouth was a regional telephone utility operating in nine southeastern states in 1984. A decade later, the company serves cellular, paging, wireline, and mobile data customers in seventeen countries on five continents.[15]

Redefinition Remedy 3 closes this chapter on market definition dimensions. Take a few minutes now to think about how your organization might apply the 3-D and 5-D approaches to better define your markets. Next, schedule a meeting with your top marketing executives to effectively respond to this thought-provoking management challenge.

SUMMARY

The dynamic nature of industrial and technology markets requires marketing executives to reassess (and redefine, as necessary) markets on a regular basis. The 3-D "plus two" approach—customer groups (market segments), customer functions (needs), technologies, competition, and products—ensures that market definitions are multidimensional and effective. In the next chapter, we will evaluate the best strategies for defining customer-based and competitive-driven markets.

REDEFINITION REMEDY 3:
USING THE 3-D AND 5-D MODELS
TO DEFINE YOUR MARKET*

1. Clarify the relevant options for defining your market. Allocate 100 points to your market definition dimensions.

Points

_____ a. Identify the potential customer needs in your market.

_____ b. Identify the potential customer groups (segments) likely to be found in your market.

_____ c. Identify the potential technologies that can be expected in your market.

_____ d. Identify the typical products requested by customers in your market.

_____ e. Identify the competitive product offerings in your market.

Total = 100

2. Using the three-dimensional market definition map (see Figure 3.6), plot potential customer needs and the two next most important dimensions for your market.

Management Challenge

- Select a primary and secondary market definition for your company. Both of these three-dimensional choices are areas to initially concentrate your marketing efforts to determine which are suitable for your organization given its capabilities, objectives, resources, and competitive situation.
- Discuss your unique selling proposition (USP) and competitive advantage for attacking these markets.

---

* Ideally, the relevant market works best (see Chapter 2).

FIGURE 3.6. Market Definition Map

Using the three-dimensional market definition map (below), plot potential customer needs and the two next most important dimensions for your market.

Market Name_____

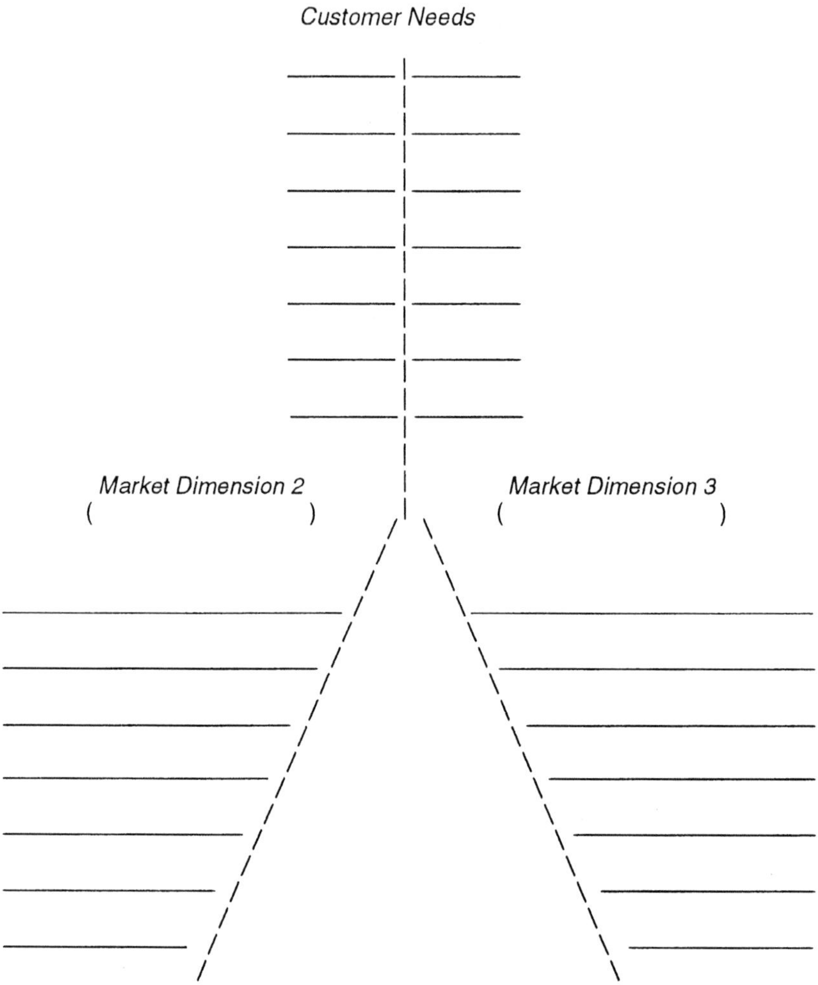

Customer Needs

_____ | _____

_____ | _____

_____ | _____

_____ | _____

_____ | _____

_____ | _____

_____ | _____

Market Dimension 2   *Market Dimension 3*
(   )   (   )

Chapter 4

Customer- and Competitive-Based Market Definitions

The dinosaur's eloquent lesson is that if some bigness is good, an overabundance of bigness is not necessarily better.

—Eric Johnston

We have two separate divisions—distinctly different industries. One is medical, the other industrial. Both are "niche" type at present. What one division does, the other may not. It all depends on our objectives and other factors.

—Vice President of Marketing and Sales, medical equipment firm

The crux of strategy formulation is market definition. Jain states that the strategic 3 Cs—customer, competition, and company (e.g., strengths, weaknesses, opportunities, and threats)—must be properly assessed to define a business.[1] Markets should be defined from both internal (within the organization) and external perspectives (competitive-based view). A balanced approach is advocated to provide the richest and most valuable market definition.

Consider how market definition impacts overall business strategy. Compaq Computer recently transformed itself from a PC company to a more diversified computer and related industries manufacturer. The company now has four core businesses: desktops and portables, consumer PCs, enterprise systems (servers and high-performance work stations), and communications products such as networking hardware and software.[2] Compaq's major challenge now is how to deal with Dell, a company that has a significant cost advantage and closer ties with its customers via its direct sales marketing strategy.

Although Canon is internationally renowned for the quality of its cameras, this Japanese giant has six other major product lines—copying machines, computers and peripherals, communication systems, personal information products, media and chemical components, and optical equipment. Although Compaq and Canon each market hundreds of individual products globally, their product mixes fit the strategic objectives of their respective organizations.

According to David Francis, Managing Principal of Mercator Consultants LLC, companies are overtaken by new competitors because they do not see the problem, believe it is real, or take action until it is too late. He adds that typical responses by complacent companies are: "We're not in that business," "Their products have limited appeal," "They're only at the bottom of the market," "We can't afford to do business their way," "That's not an attractive business for us," and/or "Those competitors are unfair."[3]

From a market definition perspective, the discounting of new competition has a substantial impact on how the organization copes with unfamiliar rivals. Remember, today's start-up may grow up to become tomorrow's Microsoft or Southwest Airlines. Just over twenty years ago, Microsoft was Bill Gates, Paul Allen, and a few dozen employees. Today, it is the king of the computer software market.

Southwest has prospered and profited for more than twenty-five years by being in the "business of freedom." Chief Executive Officer Herb Kelleher's goal is to help people fly who might not afford to or choose to via traditional routes and options. Since its average flight is less than 400 miles, Southwest often competes with automobiles, buses, and trains, rather than other airline carriers, for customers' transportation dollars.

Major differences are evidenced by market definition approaches used by executives in small firms and larger companies. Small business owners and managers typically use corporate and product line market definitions, although divisional organizational structures are, at times, beneficial.

Marketing executives in larger companies utilize a more varied approach to satisfying customer needs (e.g., product, product line, strategic business unit, and division) and responding to competition (e.g., industry, strategic groups, generic market, and product market). In addition, the job scope of the decision maker (i.e., level of management, position, and decision-making authority) has a significant impact on how markets are defined.

DEFINING CUSTOMER AND COMPETITIVE MARKETS

Holland and Knight is the largest law firm in Florida. Recently, they announced expansion plans to form a business consulting division. While they may be the first law firm to enter this arena, this decision was carefully made based on customer and competitive factors. First, their clients were asking for more than just legal services. Second, accounting firms have embraced this concept and succeeded in a big way (case in point, Andersen Consulting). Holland and Knight has ambitious plans for their new business unit; they expect it to become their largest division within the next few years.[4]

Firms are not limited to a unidimensional view of a market. Companies can often benefit by accepting multiple market definitions suitable for particular marketing management purposes (e.g., analyzing the feasibility of new ventures, corporate resource allocation, product positioning, segmentation, strategic planning, etc.). Product development teams need a longer-term strategic outlook than advertising/promotions managers. Hence, market definitions must be consistent with a firm's overall business activities.

Furthermore, market analysis should explicitly assess and anticipate customer needs and competitive strategies. A bottom-up perspective emphasizes customer requirements and usage patterns, while a top-down approach evaluates competitive capabilities and sustainable advantage.[5] Market redefinitions should be conceptualized to: (1) satisfy customer needs (i.e., internal market definitions), (2) respond to competitive pressures (i.e., external market definitions), or (3) meet both customer and competitive challenges.

A dichotomy by firm size—small versus nonsmall (medium and large companies)—yields important market redefinition insights for growing and giant companies. Relevant terminology utilized in this market definition research are operationalized in Figure 4.1.Three

FIGURE 4.1. Market Definition Terminology

Market Size Dichotomy

Small Firms—annual sales of less than $10 million
Nonsmall Firms—medium and large companies with annual sales of $10 million or higher

Usage Groups for Internal and External Market Definitions

Nonusers—executives never use a specific market definition (e.g., internal corporate)
Occasional users—executives sometimes use a specific market definition for an internal (e.g., corporate) or external (e.g., diversified) market
Regular users—executives often or always use a specific market definition for an internal (e.g., corporate) or external market (e.g., diversified)

RQ3. Internal Market Definitions: customer-driven

Corporate—relates to the entire company
Division—major part of a company (e.g., West Coast or medical instrumentation divisions)
Strategic Business Unit (SBU)—separate profit center within a division
Product Line—set of closely related products
Product/Brand—a distinct unit (good or service) offered

RQ4. External Market Definitions: competitive-driven

Diversified—cuts across two or more industries
Industry—a branch of trade (e.g., the computer industry)
Industry Sector—part of an industry (e.g., microcomputers)
Strategic Groups—a set of competitors following similar strategies (e.g., IBM and Apple)
Generic Market—customers with similar needs but differing ways of satisfying them (e.g., business communication)
Product Market—customers with similar ways of satisfying needs (e.g., fax machines)
Standard Industrial Classification (SIC) Codes—a U.S. government-derived system for categorizing industries

RQ5. Job Scope

Upper Management—president, CEO, owner, or vice president
Middle-Level Marketing Management—marketing director, division manager, marketing manager, sales manager, product manager, other marketing titles

research questions are posed to assess the approaches that firms use to define internal and external markets. These are listed in Figure 4.2.

The first query considers customer-oriented market definitions. RQ3 tests five levels of internal market definition: corporate, division, strategic business unit (SBU), product line, and product/brand. Seven types of external market definitions are evaluated in RQ4: diversified, industry, industry sector, strategic groups, generic market, product market, and Standard Industrial Classification (SIC) codes. In both cases, market definitions are analyzed via three usage groups—nonusers, occasional users, and regular users. RQ5 ex-

"Industry Survey"

Source: Dilbert® by Scott Adams, United Feature Syndicate, May 5 - May 10, 1997. Reprinted by permission.

FIGURE 4.2. Internal and External Market Definitions—Research Questions

RQ3: Do executives in small firms differ significantly from marketing executives in nonsmall firms with respect to the usage of types of internal/customer-driven market definitions?

RQ4: Do executives in small firms differ significantly from marketing executives in nonsmall firms with respect to the usage of types of external/competitive market definitions?

RQ5: Do small firms differ significantly from nonsmall firms with respect to the impact of job scope issues (i.e., level of management, responsibility, and joint decision making) on market definition?

plores the job scope of the individual defining the market (i.e., the impact of management level, position, and joint decision making on market definition) for the two subsamples.

INTERNAL/CUSTOMER DEFINITIONS

Typical internal market definitions include corporate, division, SBU, product line, and product. These approaches are derived from the three levels of market definition identified in Figure 2.1 (corporate, business, and program) and are relatively easy to employ and evaluate for effectiveness.

As shown in Table 4.1 (RQ3), statistically significant differences ($p < .05$) were found based on four of the five internal levels

TABLE 4.1. Customer-Driven Market Definitions

RQ3. Internal (Within the Firm) Market Definition:

Strategic Level	Percent Regular Users	Percent Occasional Users	Percent Nonusers
	SM, N-S (All)	SM, N-S (All)	SM, N-S (All)
ns Corporate	71, 55 (63)	15, 28 (21)	14, 17 (15)
* Product Line	47, 65 (55)	16, 18 (17)	37, 17 (28)
** Product/ Brand	33, 43 (37)	15, 28 (21)	52, 29 (41)
** Division	21, 57 (37)	14, 17 (15)	65, 26 (47)
** SBU	21, 47 (33)	10, 18 (14)	69, 34 (53)

Notes:

1. SM: small firms, < $10 million annual sales
   N-S: medium/large, ≥ $10 million annual sales

2. Percentages for each strategic level are totaled across and due to rounding approximate 100 percent.

3. Chi-square tests were computed based on three usage groups. Statistically significant differences between small and nonsmall firms are as follows:

   ** $p < .01$

   * $p < .05$

   ns not significant

(corporate was the lone exception).[6] Larger companies tended to use product line, product/brand, division, and SBU definitions more often than small companies. For example, many large banks are now quite active (and successful) in the mutual fund, securities, and annuities businesses. They are redefining themselves as *money managers* via new financial product offerings, support services such as financial advisement, and innovative delivery methods.[7]

In recent years, General Motors, IBM, Kodak, and others faced "bigness" problems caused by complacency, inbred management, and nimble global competitors. How can companies with multibillion dollar revenues avoid decline? The answer is strategic redirection, which may include entering new businesses or launching "second generation" companies.[8] These independent ventures do not suffer from their parents' bureaucracies, long-standing traditions, and entrenched business cultures.

In contrast to larger organizations, let us consider how smaller firms fared with respect to customer-driven market definitions. Small firms had a mean usage of 1.9 internal market definitions versus 2.7 for larger companies (this is statistically meaningful at $p < .01$). Overall, corporate and product line market definitions were the most frequently cited levels within the firm—small firms generally limited themselves to those two approaches, while larger companies used a more varied approach.

For example, some small health care marketers are finding their niche in the marketplace by offering medical savings accounts or medical discount card programs to employers. Small CPA firms are learning that specialists survive. This strategy is recommended to achieve better client service, find new growth opportunities, pursue specialized market niches, and command higher fees.[9]

To gain additional insight, five analyses of variance were computed to assess executives' perceptions of how successful they felt their internal market definitions were based on the specified usage groups (nonusers, occasional users, and regular users). One marginally significant relationship was found based on division. Further analysis indicated that small firms were responsible for this effect.

Specifically, small companies that occasionally defined markets by division were perceived as more successful in defining markets than firms that never employed that organizational level. While this approach may not be realistic for the start-up "garage workshop" firm, a divisional market definition may be appropriate for a growing entrepreneurial firm. A logical divisional breakdown is by geographic region (e.g., United States versus selected international markets).

EXTERNAL/COMPETITIVE DEFINITIONS

Management should also gaze outside of the organization for market insight. External/competitive market definitions can utilize some or all of the following approaches: diversified (multi-industry), industry, industry sector, strategic groups, generic market, product market, and SIC codes. In contrast to the former set (internal market definitions), this latter group requires more time, effort, and resources to properly analyze and find a sustainable competitive advantage.

In the study, companies used external (competitive) market definitions to differing degrees. Industry definition and competitive identification is usually regarded as a trivial task; clearly, it is not.[10] As shown in Table 4.2 (RQ4), statistically significant differences between small and nonsmall companies were observed based on industry, product market, strategic groups, and generic market. Small firms had a mean usage of 4.7 external market definitions versus 5.3 for larger companies (this is statistically meaningful at $p < .01$). Overall, the three most frequently used approaches were industry (e.g., computer hardware), industry sector (e.g., microcomputers), and product market (e.g., laptop computers). Based on the percentage of regular users for these approaches, a progression from most general to most specific external market definition was evidenced.

Research by the U.S. government on the fastest-growing industries for the next decade projects that the dominant firms will vary by size. For example, it is reported that large companies will lead in the manufacturing of computer equipment and semiconductors. These companies have the necessary capital to invest substantially in plant and equipment, a requirement for large-scale production. In contrast, small firms are expected to dominate many business and service sectors; this includes computer/data processing, health services, and residential care.[11] The strength of small firms in the service sector is due to entrepreneurial enthusiasm and skills, creativity, and flexibility (human capital is the critical success factor).

TABLE 4.2. Competitive-Driven Market Definitions

RQ4. Internal (Within the Firm) Market Definition:

Strategic Level	Percent Regular Users	Percent Occasional Users	Percent Nonusers
	SM, N-S (All)	SM, N-S (All)	SM, N-S (All)
* Industry	55, 68 (61)	21, 17 (19)	24, 14 (19)
ns Industry Sector	54, 60 (57)	21, 20 (21)	25, 19 (23)
** Product Market	46, 63 (54)	29, 20 (25)	25, 16 (21)
* Strategic Groups	42, 53 (46)	26, 28 (27)	32, 19 (26)
*Generic Market	35, 48 (41)	31, 34 (32)	34, 17 (26)
ns Diversified	36, 35 (35)	30, 33 (31)	34, 32 (33)
ns SIC Codes	11, 14 (12)	29, 30 (30)	60, 56 (58)

Notes:

1. SM: small firms, < $10 million annual sales
   N-S: medium/large, $\geq$ $10 million annual sales
2. Percentages for each strategic level are totaled across and due to rounding approximate 100 percent
3. Chi-square tests were computed based on three usage groups. Statistically significant differences between small and nonsmall firms are as follows:

   ** $p < .01$

   * $p < .05$

     ns not significant

AN INTEGRATIVE VIEW: USING PRODUCT-CUSTOMER MATRICES

What approaches does your company currently use to define markets? How effective are these methods? Redefinition Remedy 4 takes a critical look at your business and helps you build stronger definitions of your market from a customer and competitive perspective. This provides the necessary foundation for developing successful marketing strategies.

Product-customer matrices can provide a useful summary tool for strategic marketing planning purposes. This analytical approach helps define market boundaries and segments, matches product offerings with current customers, identifies areas of key competitors' strength (those competing in your strategic group), provides a positioning strategy map, and notes potential underserved gaps in the market.[12] An example of a product-customer matrix is depicted in Table 4.3.

JOB SCOPE AND MARKET DEFINITION

An analysis of respondents' job scope yielded interesting findings relevant to internal market definition (see Table 4.4). Typically, market definition was an upper-management decision (vice president or higher). Since management of larger companies is more specialized, it is not surprising that 60 percent of top executives make market definition decisions while 90 percent of those in similar positions in small companies handle this responsibility.

In addition, small firms were nearly four times as likely (53 percent versus 14 percent) as nonsmall companies to assign market definition decisions to the president, CEO, or owner. Larger companies tend to delegate market definition duties to vice presidents or middle-level managers.

The autonomy of market definition decision making was also assessed. While both the small and nonsmall companies clearly favor joint decisions within the firm (86 percent and 95 percent, respectively), the former group is somewhat more autocratic than the latter. This marginally significant difference may be due to the limited number of managers working in smaller firms. For example, many new and small companies may have only one executive in charge of all of the marketing activities.

SUMMARY

Market definition is a pivotal component of marketing strategy for business, service, and technology-based firms. Multinational

TABLE 4.3. Product-Customer Matrix for a Gas Supplier

Customers **Pro-ducts**	Environmental Protection		Refining, Cutting, & Binding Metals		Other Industries	
	Pulp & paper	Petro-chemi-cals	Heavy indus-tries	Light indus-tries	Medical service	Food & bever-age
Bulk oxygen	B, D		B, D		A, B, C, D	
Oxygen in cyl-inders	A, B, C, D		B, C, D	B, C, D	B, C, D	
Oxygen, on-site	B, D		A			
Bulk nitro-gen	B, D	A, B, D	B			B, C
Spec-ialty gases	B, C, D	A, B, D	B, D	A, B, D	A, B, D	B, C, D
Fuel gases	B, C, D		B, C, D	**B, C, D**		
Carbon dioxide	B, C		B, D	B, C, D		B, C
Welding	B, C, D		B, C, D	**B, C, D**		

Key: A = client firm; B, C, D = competitors
   B, C, D = companies in the largest product-customer segments

Source: Boardman, Anthony E. and Vining, Aidan R. "Defining Your Business Using Product-Customer Matrices," *Long-Range Planning*, 29(1), 1996, pp. 38-48.

TABLE 4.4. Job Scope and Market Definition

Variable	Total Sample	Small Firms	Nonsmall Firms	Chi-Square
Management Level Responsible for Market Definition	202	110	92	32.8 ***
Upper	154	99	55	
Middle	48	11	37	
No Response	1	0	1	
Individual Responsible for Market Definition	198	108	90	25.25 ***
Pres./CEO/Owner	70	57	13	
Vice President	61	25	36	
Midlevel Mktg.	58	21	37	
Nonmarketing	9	5	4	
No Response	5	2	3	
Joint Decisions in Defining Markets	202	110	92	3.78 #
Yes	182	95	87	
No	20	15	5	
No Response	1	0	1	

Key: *** $p < .001$
 # $p < .10$

companies as well as fledgling entrepreneurs must cope with this crucial business decision.

Take the case of AT&T's recent restructuring (the "trivestiture") as an example. Management proclaims that AT&T is no longer a long-distance telephone company or even a telecommunications company. Rather, it is competing in the multitrillion-dollar global information industry. Its three stand-alone companies—AT&T (the services businesses), Lucent Technologies (the new systems and technology company), and NCR (the computer company)—have multibillion-dollar businesses and are customer focused on key industry sectors.[13] Smaller telecommunications competitors may require more specialized market definitions relating to mobile communications technologies, public pay phone and related services, and so on.

A clear understanding of the best ways to define customer and competitive-driven markets can lead to improved business performance. In this chapter, the usage frequency, value, and potential applications of internal and external market definitions was examined. In the next chapter, we turn our attention to market selection, segmentation, and target marketing strategies.

REDEFINITION REMEDY 4:
CUSTOMER AND COMPETITIVE MARKET DEFINITIONS

A. *Internal (Customer-Driven) Market Definitions*

1. Our *corporate* market definition is:

2. Our *divisions* are:

3. Our *SBUs* are:

4. Our *product lines* are:

5. Our *products/services* include:

Management Challenge

- We need to revise the following internal approaches to improve our market definition: _____
  _____
  _____

- We should think about using the following internal approaches to improve our market definition:_____
  _____
  _____

- The business implications of redefining your internal markets are as follows:

  1. _____
  2. _____
  3. _____
  4. _____
  5. _____

B. *External (Competitive-Driven) Market Definitions*

1. Our *diversified* market definition is:

2. Our *industry* is:

3. Our *industry sectors* are:

4. Our *strategic groups* include:

5. Our *generic market* includes:

6. Our *product markets* are:

7. Our *SIC codes* are:

Management Challenge

- We need to revise the following external approaches to improve our market definition:_____

_____

_____

- We should think about using the following external approaches to improve our market definition:_____

_____

_____

- The business implications of redefining our external markets are as follows:

    1. _____

    2. _____

    3. _____

    4. _____

    5. _____

Chapter 5

Defining and Segmenting Business Markets

You can't be all things to all people. But I can be all things to people I select.

—Donald Neuenschwander

Markets are defined at three levels: basic strategies, segment strategies, and product/customer strategies.

—Vice President, electronics company

Understanding markets is critical to business success. Firms must carefully define and segment markets to find new customers and keep existing ones. Neuenschwander, the chairman of the Medical Center Bank in Houston, subscribed to this philosophy in targeting physicians and other wealthy clients. Less than 20 percent of small business customers may account for as much as 90 percent of a bank's profitability in financial services.[1]

Based on an exploratory research study of top marketing managers in nine technology-driven industries, market selection strategies and their impact on effective market definition and target marketing are analyzed in this chapter. Concentrated marketing was found to be a preferable strategy to an undifferentiated approach. Differentiated marketers were more effective target marketers than undifferentiated firms but did not differ significantly based on market definition success.

Business education and professional training in marketing related to the usage of SIC codes. The SIC system was infrequently employed, however, and not supported as a beneficial market selection tool.

MARKET SELECTION

Market selection decisions (i.e., market definition and segmentation) provide a basis for strategy formation in business markets. Marketing managers face high levels of market and technological uncertainty in markets that are fast changing and highly competitive. According to *American Demographics,* companies fail to understand their markets for to several reasons. These include: (1) neglecting core customers in favor of new ones, (2) ignoring market shifts, (3) launching products without a clear target, and (4) failing to recognize when a market peaks.[2]

Apple Computer, a firm known for its technological prowess in the 1980s but marketing shortcomings in the 1990s, has struggled time and again with market definition and segmentation issues. For example, the company was too committed to its intensely loyal Macintosh users, an important market segment, but one that accounts for less than 10 percent of the PC market. This single-minded mission to create a Mac-world at the expense of developing other profitable computer products led to the decline of the company.

Recently, Apple introduced an innovative, stylish new product called the eMate 300. This small laptop offers solid features such as e-mail, Web browsing, word processing, spreadsheet, and organizing functions. Though the product may be of great interest to business and home users, Apple again missed the market by targeting the eMate 300 exclusively to the education market.[3]

SEGMENTATION: THE KEY TO EFFECTIVE MARKETING STRATEGY

First recognized by the late Wendell Smith in the mid-1950s, market segmentation has evolved from an academic concept into a viable real-world planning strategy.[4] Segmentation means that markets can be partitioned by finding similarities in customer characteristics or purchase behavior. Hence, selected groups of customers (target markets) are likely to exhibit similar purchase behavior.

Prior to target marketing, firms relied solely on a product differentiation strategy to appeal to different customers. Product uniqueness is always a desirable objective. Product-specific factors such as type of market (e.g., original equipment manufacturer versus aftermarket), price-quality relationships, distribution/service, product quality and attributes, and technology should be integrated into a joint supply-side and demand-side approach to segmentation.[5]

The Bosch Group, a German company, is the worldwide market leader in antilocking braking systems (ABS). In the early 1990s, they focused on middle-to-higher priced automobiles and modified their systems to meet the needs of global manufacturers. An opportunity was present to target lower-priced vehicles. This relatively large market segment can be effectively served with less costly, rather standardized ABS systems. In particular, this target market is quite attractive in Japan and the United States.

The choice of markets to serve is the essence of sound strategic planning. Organizations need to determine their optimal markets based on analysis of their internal and external environments. Once a market definition has been accepted by management, it serves as the foundation upon which the marketing program (e.g., product strategy, promotional mix, pricing, and distribution) can be formulated and implemented. The concept of levels of market definition (corporate, business unit, and program) means that STP marketing—segmentation, targeting, and positioning—can only be successfully developed and implemented if a definition of the "pre-segmented" market for the SBU exists.

For more than a century, Pittsburgh-based PPG Industries has flourished as a producer of paint, glass, and chemicals. When its traditional core products began to languish, this manufacturer was forced to explore new market segments. The results were mixed. Some related, successful opportunities were found with PPG's Transitions sunglasses; glass-based computer hard disks (a replacement for aluminum components); managing automotive paint operations for Chrysler and other companies; and establishing an insurance claim network.[6]

Using Segmentation Bases to Find New Markets

Markets can be segmented in many ways. There is no one clear, best method; a lot depends on a company's market situation and information needs. In most cases, several segmentation bases need to be considered simultaneously to provide a complete customer profile.

Geographics and business demographics (also called firmographics) are generally the starting points. Behavioral approaches such as product usage analysis, benefits, buyer adopter categories, industrial psychographics, media exposure, and so on are more costly and time consuming to implement but can add greater insight to marketing situations. A list of ten important segmentation bases and their associated variables, which are frequently used in business, service, and technology markets is shown in Figure 5.1.[7]

Source: Dilbert® by Scott Adams, United Feature Syndicate, October 3-October 8, 1994. Reprinted by permission.

MARKET DEFINITION AND SEGMENTATION: RESEARCH QUESTIONS

A marketing orientation is built on the premise of customer satisfaction via target marketing. Empirical testing of the effects of various market selection options (i.e., undifferentiated, differentiated, and concentrated marketing) is lacking, however. Industrial marketing textbooks provide anecdotal evidence recommending the use of SIC codes as a tool for segmenting and targeting business-to-business markets.[8] Although SIC codes are widely advocated, how useful is this approach in market selection decisions? Also, what impact does education and training have on the usage of this dimension? Hence, three research questions are posed in Figure 5.2.

FIGURE 5.1. Business Segmentation Bases

- Adopter Categories—innovators, early adopters, early majority, late majority, laggards
- Benefits—common buying factors
- Business Demographics—number of prospects, type of business, sales volume, employee size, years in business, etc.
- End Use—raw materials, work in process, finished goods, product applications
- Geographics—market scope and standardized/census market areas
- Loyalty—loyal versus nonloyal customers, degree of loyalty
- Price—price sensitivity/elasticity, price/quality, price incentives
- Purchasing—purchasing functions, policies, and criteria; buyer relationships
- Standard Industrial Classification codes—a U.S. government reference for defining American industries
- User Status—heavy versus medium versus light users (based on unit or dollar sales, number of orders)

FIGURE 5.2. Market Segmentation—Research Questions

RQ6: Are segmenters (single- and multiple-target marketers) more successful in defining markets than nonsegmenters (undifferentiated marketers)?

RQ7: Are segmenters (single- and multiple-target marketers) more successful in targeting markets than nonsegmenters (undifferentiated marketers)?

RQ8: How useful is the SIC approach in market selection?

MARKET SELECTION FINDINGS

Market Definition and Market Selection

To segment effectively, companies must precisely define the markets in which they compete. This process is complex and critical—particularly in high-technology markets—because it is often difficult to accurately evaluate customer needs until after products are introduced into the marketplace.

This study revealed that technology-driven companies were heavily dependent on a primary market segment which accounted for 69 percent of their business.[9] Since the key segment is so influential, firms must carefully assess market selection decisions. In an attempt to do basically one thing extremely well (and profitably), many doctors and hospitals now focus on specialties such as back care, cancer treatment, coronary care, or wellness programs. In a recent study, Astra/Merck targeted doctors based on the following physician profile: medical thought leaders, cost-sensitive physicians, traditionalists, and health care as a business providers.

The segmentation/targeting approach used by industrial and high-tech firms was evaluated. Nearly two-thirds of the companies (65 percent) used a differentiation strategy, serving two or more target markets with unique marketing programs. For example, in the mini-computer market, Hewlett-Packard's proprietary HP 3000 appeals to the availability/performance and solution/service target markets, while their HP 9000, a Unix-designed system, was designed for the transparent access (early adopters, network users) and value segments (price sensitive, smaller companies).[10]

A variation of differentiated segmentation may be based on the buyer phase of the purchase decision process—e.g., first time prospects, novices (new customers), and sophisticates (established customers).[11] GTE knows that its customers' buying motives may vary considerably; start-ups generally seek technical guidance and service, while established firms are often interested in customized new products and service advancements. GTE's diversified but consistent strategies in all important sectors of the telecommunications industry (local, long distance, on-line, and wireless) is the reason that some analysts have called GTE the phone company of the future. In actuality, they are evolving into a data communications and networking enterprise.[12]

The balance of the firms were split fairly evenly between an undifferentiated approach (18 percent) and a concentrated strategy (17 percent). While the net effect of undifferentiated and concentrated marketing appears to be the same (the development of only one marketing program), the two methods are vastly different, conceptually and pragmatically. Undifferentiated marketers use the Henry Ford approach (give customers anything they want, provided it's a black Model-T), while focused marketers subscribe to the Colonel Sanders/KFC philosophy (do only one thing, but do it right).

Hidden champions are often obscure companies that become market leaders by doing one thing exceptionally well. For example, Minneapolis-based St. Jude is seven times larger than its nearest competitor by focusing almost exclusively on heart valves; Amorim, a Portuguese company, is the world leader in wine corks; and Krones AG, a German company, manufactures beverage-labeling machines.[13]

As the analysis of variance (ANOVA) and post hoc comparison test in Table 5.1 indicates, firms utilizing a concentrated strategy (a narrow, well-defined, single-customer segment) were significantly more successful in defining markets than undifferentiated firms (mass marketers). Somewhat surprising was that there was no statistically significant difference found between undifferentiated

TABLE 5.1. Market Definition Success* by Market Selection Strategy

Source	Degrees of Freedom	Sum of Squares	Mean Squares	F-test/ P-value
Between groups	2	5.37	2.69	4.67/ .01
Within groups	198	113.85	.58	
TOTAL	200	119.22		

Groups	Count	Mean	Standard Deviation	Standard Error
Undiffer-entiated	36	3.13	.90	.15
Concen-trated	35	3.67	.86	.14
Differen-tiated	130	3.43	.69	.06
TOTAL	201	3.42	.77	.05

Tukey's HSD test: groups 1 and 2 are significantly different at the .05 level.
*Measure: "Our firm's market definitions are successful." (1 = strongly disagree to 5 = strongly agree)

and differentiated marketers with respect to market definition success. Hence, RQ6 received mixed support.

Target Marketing and Market Selection

Research Question 7 was clearly supported. As Table 5.2 illustrates, segmenters (firms using a concentrated or a differentiated strategy) were more effective target marketers than undifferentiated firms (non-segmenters). The value of the rifle (target marketing) over the shotgun approach (mass marketing) is evidenced. Based on this research, a single target market strategy is clearly superior to an undifferentiated one.

Companies using a mass marketing strategy can benefit by switching to concentrated target marketing. In particular, entrepre-

TABLE 5.2. Target Marketing Success* by Market Selection Strategy

Source	Degrees of Freedom	Sum of Squares	Mean Squares	F-test/ P-value
Between groups	2	15.50	7.75	7.18/ .001
Within groups	198	211.56	1.08	
TOTAL	200	227.06		

Groups	Count	Mean	Standard Deviation	Standard Error
Undiffer- entiated	35	2.71	1.25	.21
Concen- trated	35	3.40	1.14	.19
Differen- tiated	129	3.45	.94	.08
TOTAL	199	3.32	1.07	.08

Tukey's HSD test: group 1 is significantly different from groups 2 and 3 at the .05 level. *Measure: "How successful is your firm in target marketing?" (1 = unsuccessful to 5 = very successful)

neurial firms with limited resources are likely to gain from a focused strategy. Managers must carefully evaluate their objectives, corporate strengths and weaknesses, market size, growth rate, profit potential, competition, and other firm- and industry-specific factors in choosing an appropriate target market. Firms that are successful with a single target market strategy or with a carefully conceived multiple target market approach may also investigate niche markets for new profit opportunities.

In addition, some diversified organizations may consider streamlining their operations and reducing the number of markets in which they compete. This strategy worked effectively for Cordis Corporation, a Miami-based medical device manufacturer and distributor (now part of Johnson & Johnson). A divestiture of their financially ailing pacemaker division helped restore profitability to the company. Cordis enhanced its worldwide market leadership position in the cardiac catheter business as a result.

Recently, Ivax announced that it is selling its McGaw intravenous products unit to Germany's B. Braun Melsungen AG as part of its strategy to concentrate on its core pharmaceuticals business.[14] It is interesting to note that Robert C. Strauss engineered divestitures of both Cordis and Ivax in his leadership position as president of these companies, at two distinct points in time.

SIC Analysis and Market Selection

Standard Industrial Classification codes, a Census Bureau tool, are frequently recommended as a technique for analyzing market and competitive structures.[15] Since product complementarity and technological association are clearly significant in many SIC categories, such codes are a useful starting point for defining and targeting markets.[16] This approach may be especially valuable when there are no strong demand-side factors delineating market boundaries. Furthermore, SIC analysis helps industrial managers avoid the error of drawing market boundaries too narrowly.

SIC codes are subject, however, to some key limitations. First, four through seven digit industry codes are inconsistent (often too broad or narrow) and may be problematic when exclusively used for market selection. Second, SIC data does not necessarily correspond to actual geographic market boundaries. It assumes all markets are domestic and neglects import competition. Third, infrequent updates (every ten years or so) are a major problem in dynamic growth markets.

In spite of these shortcomings, SIC analysis can provide a useful "first cut" approach to segmentation. For example, a national uniform supply company buys seven-digit Dun & Bradstreet SIC data on computer tape and CD-ROM and targets channel end users by industry type. For example, approximately 80 percent of their sales are rental uniforms to laundries, 15 percent to end users, and 5 percent direct.

In this investigation, only 12 percent of the managers relied on SIC codes as a method for defining competitive markets on a regular basis (often or always used this approach in market selection decisions). Thirty percent of the firms occasionally used SIC codes, while 58 percent never used this approach. Despite its widespread endorsement in the industrial marketing and economics literature, a majority of technology-based managers do not tap this potentially valuable source of marketing information.

It is likely that these executives were not exposed to SIC analysis since most were not formally educated in business (63 percent of the respondents earned undergraduate degrees in nonbusiness disciplines—e.g., engineering, sciences, etc.). As expected, a chi-square test between SIC usage (never, occasional, and regular) and college education (none, nonbusiness, business, and marketing) was statistically significant, $p < .04$.

Similarly, these managers had limited professional training in marketing (e.g., American Marketing Association programs, Burke Marketing Research seminars, executive education, etc.). The mean number of on-the-job training courses varied by SIC usage category (never = 2.9, occasional = 5.2, regular = 3.5). The one-way ANOVA was significant, $p < .03$.

Although it was possible to profile SIC users by educational and professional training, the value of SIC analysis as a market selection tool was not supported. There were no statistically significant differences found between nonusers, occasional users, and regular users of SIC codes and market definition success. In addition, a chi-square test by SIC usage level and target marketing strategy employed (undifferentiated, differentiated, and concentrated) was also nonsignificant.

Perhaps these findings indicate that SIC codes need to be used in conjunction with other industrial segmentation dimensions to be effective, rather than just used in isolation. Bonoma and Shapiro's five-component nested approach (demographics, operating variables, purchasing approach, situational factors, and personal characteristics) is one such integrative model that stresses the need for multiple segmentation bases.[17] Redefinition Remedy 5 helps ensure that firms are using several segmentation dimensions to best understand their market situations.

In sum, more detailed general and proprietary coding systems are needed for business marketing situations. SIC market analysis does not have to be abandoned. Rather, its limitations and applications (i.e., role as a supplemental business demographic variable) can be stressed by marketing educators and practitioners. Also, marketers should be aware that a major overhaul of the SIC system is being undertaken at this time. The revised coding scheme is called the North American Industry Classification System (NAICS). Check the U.S. government's Census Bureau Web page for further details—www.census.gov/epcd/www/naics.html.

SUMMARY

The research discussed in this chapter supports the value of target marketing in business and high technology markets. Although a target marketing strategy is desirable, the "right" market selection option varies by firm. Both concentrated and differentiated strategies can be effective. Firms should carefully assess their resources, capabilities, market opportunities, and competitive environment in their decision process.

The interrelation of market definition and segmentation must also be recognized. Industries are constantly undergoing change. Companies that were successful in defining markets were also likely to be successful in segmentation/targeting activities ($r = .58$, $p < .01$). Therefore, marketers must first grasp how to define presegmented markets. The 3-D model and 5-D extension discussed in Chapter 3 provide an excellent starting point for exploring market definition and segmentation decisions. In the next chapter, we will deal with a big issue, market redefinition.

REDEFINITION REMEDY 5:
BUSINESS SEGMENTATION DIMENSIONS*

1. How do you define your market geographically?
   How could you define your market geographically?

2. Describe your target market(s) by the following business demographic variables: type of business, sales volume, number of employees, number of locations, number of years in business, market position.

3. Can you identify key user categories (e.g., heavy versus light users, loyal versus nonloyal customers, user-group needs, geographic discrepancies)?

4. Have you assessed key benefit segments?
   What are the common buying factors present in the market?

5. Are other behavioral segmentation dimensions (that is, industrial psychographics, perceptions, media exposure, marketing mix factors) relevant and used in your analysis?

6. Have you identified and researched your target markets by SIC code?

7. Have you conducted a product end-use analysis?

8. How can you apply adopter category segmentation to your market situation?

9. Are your target markets based on segmentation research?

10. Are multiple business segmentation bases used?

Management Challenge

- The segmentation objective is threefold: (1) to retain and upgrade relationships with current customers, (2) to find new customers, and (3) to win back former users. By successfully answering the above ten questions, you will be closer to accomplishing these three key business goals.

---

* Source: Weinstein, Art. *Market Segmentation: Using Demographics, Psychographics, and Other Niche Marketing Techniques to Predict Customer Behavior,* Revised Edition (Irwin, Burr Ridge, IL, 1994, p. 172).

Chapter 6

Market Redefinition Guidelines

There's a certain amount of disorder that has to be reorganized.

—William S. Paley

New market segments, products, and services are continuously reviewed and redefined.

—Vice President of Marketing and Sales,
photonics company

Business, service, and technology firms define their markets in many ways. How successful are these market views? When and how should market definitions be revised? For example, of seven redefinition strategies tested, changing customer needs was found to be the most effective approach, while changing customer segments was least effective. Key motivations for market redefinition were management decision, technology, market/competitive analysis, and low sales. On average, markets were redefined (this means a change in customer needs, segments, or technologies occurred) about every two years. These and related issues are explored in this chapter.

CHANGE IS THE ONLY CONSTANT IN BUSINESS

Rapid change and market uncertainty in business markets implies that successful firms are responsive and proactive with respect to their market environments. As their markets have changed, many accounting firms have entered the business consulting arena. This evolution has spawned such innovative ventures as "Ernie" (Ernst

& Young's Internet consulting service, aimed at small business clients); Boulay, Heutmaker, Zibell & Company's "virtual corporation group" consisting of independent service providers in various areas of business expertise; and industry-specific accounting firms, among other strategic initiatives and redirections.[1]

Microsoft caught Encyclopedia Brittanica asleep at the wheel when it offered a CD-ROM encyclopedia. The salesforce was still pushing $2,000 print sets when a $100 computerized option had become available. Brittanica recently switched from a consumer to an institutional market focus, and they have responded effectively by continual updating their new electronic products.

Andy Grove, chairperson of Intel, notes that companies win or lose in the marketplace based on their degree of adaptability. He adds that companies face strategic inflection points due to dramatic shifts in the competitive picture, technology, customer behaviors, and other market discontinuities or drivers. The strategic inflection point means that business fundamentals are about to change and the company will be presented with great opportunities or the beginning of its end.[2] How well the firm faces this pivotal period will ultimately determine its success or failure as an enterprise. A list of four technology-based companies and their response to change is shown in Table 6.1.

REDEFINING MARKETS: ISSUES

Initially, two aspects of market redefinition are evaluated: (1) the frequency with which business firms define markets and, (2) which redefinition strategies are most/least successful. Later, we will consider management's motivations and related strategic considerations for market redefinition.

Abell proposed seven alternative strategies for market redefinition based on changes in customer groups (segments), customer functions (needs), and technologies.[3] This conceptualization is quite important but was not previously empirically tested. The market redefinition research questions that were investigated in my study are shown in Figure 6.1.

The market redefinition RQs were measured as follows. The "number of times markets were redefined during the past five years"

Table 6.1. Companies That Have Adapted to Change

Company	Change	Action	Result
AT&T	Deregulation—new local, long distance, and equipment competitors	Became market and customer oriented	A fourfold increase in stock value of AT&T and the former "Baby Bells"
Lotus	Microsoft's presence in application software	Deemphasized spreadsheets and developed Notes business	IBM purchased company for $3.5 billion
Intel	Japanese forced company out of memory chips business	Entered relatively new field, micro-processors	Company returned to profitability
Next	Windows-based PCs dominated market	Became a software company	Survived as a small niche company

Source: Adapted from Grove, Andrew S. *Only the Paranoid Survive* (New York: Currency/Doubleday, 1996).

FIGURE 6.1. Market Redefinition—Research Questions

RQ9: Do firms perceived as successful in defining markets redefine them more often than less successful firms?

RQ10: Is there a relationship between market redefinition strategies selected and perceived success in defining markets?

was correlated with "market definition success" to examine the direction and strength of the relationship postulated in RQ9. A three-item dichotomous (yes/no) scale, "When your firm last redefined the market, did you change: (1) customer groups, (2) customer functions, and/or (3) technologies?" yielded information on seven possible market redefinition strategies. This procedure operationalized

Abell's conceptualization of how markets are redefined. Market definition success was used as the dependent variable in RQ10.

REDEFINING MARKETS: INSIGHTS

Market redefinition is a crucial strategic decision for organizations; clearly, it is not an exercise for executives to take lightly. The strategic window concept states that a careful analysis and choice of various redefinition options is essential for capitalizing on the timing, resources, and capabilities fit between a firm and its defined market (and potential business opportunities).[4]

The need to change the fundamental way a firm chooses to do business makes an important statement to all of its stakeholders— shareholders, employees, customers, and so on. Redefining markets means getting out of declining businesses as well as jumping into new opportunities (following careful analysis) that are presented.

Motorola is an excellent case in point. This electronics giant exited from its successful television business in the 1960s to pursue a new strategic direction that better meshed with its corporate vision. Under the Galvin family leadership, Motorola has become a leader in the communications (e.g., cellular/wireless, paging, modems, mobile, and messaging products), semiconductor, and electronic components markets.

While some industry analysts have expressed recent concern about the possible erosion of Motorola's core businesses and the lack of breakthrough products on the horizon, historically this company has successfully met market redefinition challenges head-on, and ultimately prospered. In fact, their formula for continual reinvention is worthy of emulation. The three key points upon which their transformation processes are based are:

- generate a knowledge base to project where and how to best leverage core competencies;
- constantly search for how to better your product lines, processes, and people; and
- have the courage and passion to reinvent your company or product line.[5]

It is interesting to note that research found that high-growth companies such as CNN, Direct Line Insurance, and Starbucks paid relatively little attention to the competition. Instead, they try to make the competition irrelevant by relentlessly creating superior value for their customers. This can be accomplished by questioning everything an industry and competitors are doing, and truly understanding what customers value.[6]

Dell Computer is the prototypical strategic innovator. Building on its direct marketing expertise, the company now sells PCs and equipment to the tune of more than two million dollars a day via its Internet Web site. And more than 80 percent of these buyers are new customers.[7]

Market Redefinition Frequency

Adaptability and effectiveness (e.g., market definition success) are important performance dimensions to top executives and business unit managers. Adaptability is the organization's success in responding to changing environmental conditions over a designated period—five years is a commonly used time frame.[8]

On average, technology markets were redefined 2.5 times in the past five years, with the last redefinition occurring two years ago. Fifteen percent of the firms did not redefine their market, while 63 percent changed their market definition within the past year. One marketer commented that his market was redefined continuously; another stated that his market was unchanged for twenty-one years.[9]

The information technologies market, which broadly encompasses telecommunications, computers, microprocessors, software, video, and related technologies, illustrates the convergence and complexity of markets, and the market definition dilemma. One writer concluded that supply-side forces and technical sophistication mean that the information technologies market is changing almost daily.[10] Now, that's what I call a marketing challenge!

Although anecdotal evidence suggests that high market redefinition frequency (i.e., many changes in an organization's market definition during the specified time frame) may lead to increased business performance, research results did not support this hypothesized relationship. Hence, the quality of the market definition appears to be more important than the quantity (number of times redefined).

It is always a good idea to revisit market definitions annually in conjunction with key strategic marketing planning activities such as the development of the marketing plan. If a significant event takes place in your market (e.g., a new competitor enters the market, a major competitor exits the market, regulatory change occurs, new technology is introduced, new customer needs are identified, etc.), this would also call for a review and reanalysis of the market definition.

Market Redefinition Strategies

While market redefinition frequency had little impact on business performance, the specific redefinition strategies employed were associated with market definition success. The eight strategic options tested (the seven redefinition strategies and the no-change case) and its associated market performance measures are shown in Table 6.2.

A *needs-driven* strategy (strategic option 1) was the most successful. Customer needs or functions are generally interpreted as customer benefits.[11] The **FAB** formula tells us that (Product) Fea-

Table 6.2. Market Redefinition Strategies

Redefinition Strategy	Changes in:	Count	Rank/Mean
1. Needs-driven	needs	32	1/3.70
2. Segment switchers	groups	16	8/2.97
3. Technology	technology	20	6/3.30
4. Customer-driven	needs, groups	39	3/3.46
5. Needs/ technology	needs, technology	36	2/3.58
6. Segment/ technology	groups, technology	9	4/3.44
7. Total change	needs, groups, and technologies	34	5/3.31
8. No change	no changes	15	7/3.07

tures + **A**dvantages = **B**enefits. For example, CompuRent leases a full line of state-of-the-art computers (*features*) to banks, hospitals, schools, nonprofit organizations, and industry. The *advantages* of this service include: customers can try before they buy, cash flow is controlled, and monthly payments can be applied toward purchase. The *benefit* of this service is that many small and new businesses can now utilize powerful computer equipment that they otherwise would not be able to afford.

In contrast, *segment switchers* (strategic option 2)—firms that changed market segments alone without appraising customer needs, was the least successful of the approaches tested. Surprisingly, this strategy was perceived as being even worse than inertia—*no change* (strategic option 8). A statistically significant difference was found between strategies 1 and 2 ($p < .05$).

A change in both customer groups and needs (*customer-driven* strategic option 4) yielded better results than segment switching or a *technology-driven* approach (option 3) and was the most frequently used market redefinition option (21 percent of the sample). Changing two of the three core dimensions (strategic option 4 through 6) led to increased market performance. *Total change* (option 7), the most radical strategy, was third in popularity but less successful than all of the two-dimensional adaptations.

Motivations for New Market Views

Companies evolve over time and rethink the essence of their business. For example, IBM's recent shift from the hardware side (selling computers) of their business to the software and services side is reflected in their advertising campaign "solutions for a small planet." Toshiba recently said that they were no longer a television manufacturer, but rather design home theater products.

Managers were asked to explain what prompted the changes in their current views of the market. The top five reasons markets were redefined from an internal perspective were: management decision, technology, sales below expectation, acquisition or merger, and organizational or personnel change. From an external perspective, the three most important motivations for market redefinition were market analysis, competition, and industry regulation. Overall, firms were twice as likely to use internal reasons than external factors when redefining markets. Redefinition Remedy 6 assesses the key market redefinition issues reviewed in this chapter.

SUMMARY

Today's business, service, and technology markets face rapid change and intense competition. Smart executives cope decisively and effectively with market and technological uncertainties. Strong managers know how to respond to market dynamics by reviewing market strategies and redefining markets, when necessary.

Generally, an analysis of customer needs and benefits is the first step. Customer groups and technologies (as well as products and competition) must also be reexamined on a periodic basis. Market redefinition motivations may originate within the organization (management-based) or be necessitated by market/external forces. How well does your company adapt to changing market conditions? In the next chapter, we will consider market definition from a macro-perspective (industry) and consider several proposed relationships between market conduct and performance variables.

REDEFINITION REMEDY 6:
MARKET REDEFINITION

1. Market Redefinition Frequency and Motivation

    a. How many times has your firm redefined its market during the past five years?
    b. When did your firm last redefine its market?
    c. What factors (internal or external) caused you to redefine your market?

2. Market Redefinition Strategy

    a. As summarized in Table 6.2, which of the seven basic strategies was used (i.e., needs-driven, segment switching, technology-driven, customer-driven, need/technology, segment/technology, or total change)?
    b. Add products and competition to a revised 5-D model of market redefinition and describe your most recent market redefinition by circling whether each of the core market definitions changed (yes) or not (no).

• Customer needs	YES	NO
• Customer groups	YES	NO
• Technologies	YES	NO
• Products	YES	NO
• Competition	YES	NO

Management Challenge

• What strategic changes do you need to make in your market redefinition process to improve your view of the market (the outcome)?

Chapter 7

Market Strategies and Performance

Success is more a function of consistent common sense than it is of genius.

—An Wang

An important issue is the availability and access to data related to how markets are defined.

—President, robotics manufacturer

Smart managers know that effective market definition is a critical success factor in business, service, and technology-based industries since these markets are characterized by high degrees of market and technological uncertainty. As technologies evolve, new uses are often found that supplant the original, intended applications. For example, in the late 1970s Gordon E. Moore, Intel's cofounder, felt that industrial automation, transaction processing, and telecommunciations were the best uses for its 286 chip; personal computers were not even considered! Other interesting products that succeeded in remarkably different ways than conceived include microwaves (from radar to home cooking), the Internet (from a military network designed to survive a Soviet attack to the information and communication superhighway), and Edison's phonograph (from a dictating machine for letter writers to a music playback device).[1]

In this chapter, we explore and test six market definition issues derived from an industrial organization (a branch of economics) model called the *Market Structure-Market Conduct-Market Performance* (SCP) paradigm. Our research results show that overall (aggregate) market definition success is positively related to a marketing orientation and the use of a set of market definition criteria (multidimensional, flexible, operational, and future-directed). Technological orientation, while an important issue for management, was not found to be significantly related to market definition success.

NATURAL VERSUS ENACTED MARKETS

Brooks explains that there are two types of market definitions: natural and enacted. Natural markets are shared or collective markets (a set of relevant competitors exist) within given geographic and product constraints, while enacted markets are firm-specific and reflect the outcome of management's perception of their environment.[2]

The Federal Trade Commission blocked the proposed multibillion-dollar Office Depot and Staples merger because it ruled that both companies were in the office supply superstore market (natural market). The FTC believed that this business marriage would violate antitrust guidelines by restricting competition, which would result in price increases to customers. In contrast, mail order office supply distributors such as Quill or Viking are not concerned with market structure issues; they must deal with how to best define unique markets for their businesses (enacted markets).

While both market situations must be understood, this chapter takes a macro view of market definition and concentrates on natural markets; this is consistent with the research tradition of the SCP paradigm. In the next chapter, a micro view of market definition further explores enacted markets.

MARKET DEFINITION RELATIONSHIPS

Traditional Approaches to Analyzing Markets

Practitioners and researchers have used various approaches to explore relationships among the key business/marketing variables of industry structure, firm structure, competition, strategy, and performance. In addition to marketing insights, sources of relevant business theory and their major emphases include business policy (strategy), industrial organization (market structure), and organization theory (firm structure).[3]

Health care markets provide a good case in point. Metropolitan Statistical Areas (MSAs), a U.S. Bureau of Census classification, are often used as relevant markets in assessing hospital services. Based on a recent study, the top four firm-market concentration ratios averaged 30 percent (ranging from 15 percent in Chicago to 71 percent in Westchester). Overall, 27 percent of the hospitals were classified as for-profit (with a low of 5 percent in Pittsburgh to a high of 71 percent in Houston).[4]

Companies such as Columbia/HCA, the industry leader in hospitals, can use this information in building its presence on a market-by-market basis. Similarly, Medtronic, the top manufacturer of cardiac pacemakers and related medical devices, can target specific hospitals in designated geographic regions by hospital type, bed size/occupancy rates, market share, and growth.

The market definition problem is often evaluated through behavioral (e.g., brand switching) or judgmental (e.g., similarity of evoked sets or substition in use) methods.[5] As an extreme example, one might argue that postage stamps, e-mail service, long-distance telephone calls, videoconferencing, and airline tickets are all competitive offerings.

While substitution-based approaches help clarify market structure/buying decisions, they have three shortcomings: (1) they are product oriented, (2) they fail to explicitly consider relationships among competition, marketing and business strategy, and performance, and (3) they tend to be geared to consumer markets. Hence, an alternative approach is advocated.

Market Definition and the Structure-Conduct-Performance Approach

Industrial organization insights were used to develop a market definition research framework that provides a basis for discussion. The *structure* → *conduct* → *performance* (SCP) framework provides a conceptual basis for evaluating market definition in industrial and technology markets. The unifying thread for SCP theory is that the subject matter is confined to business organizations, market and industry structures, marketing and related strategies, and business performance.[6] Therefore, the set of variables derived for strategic planning research or a productivity assessment will differ from those needed for an analysis of market definition.

The SCP trichotomy states that market performance depends on the conduct of firms operating in a given market, and conduct depends upon the structure of that market.[7] Market structure can be reflected by the competitiveness of a market. Conduct refers to marketing behavior (e.g., implementing a marketing orientation; segmenting, targeting, and positioning; and executing marketing mix activities) and business strategy decisions (e.g., R & D commitments, plant investment, etc.). Performance can be viewed from a micro- (firm) or macro- (societal) perspective.

The SCP paradigm has received limited attention in marketing. However, Lusch and Laczniak adopted SCP methodology to explain marketing strategy issues (competition and business performance).[8] They explain that marketers often examine constructs that can be derived from SCP theory. While economists focus on structure issues, marketers are most interested in the conduct (strategy) of competing firms in the marketplace.

AN SCP MARKET DEFINITION MODEL

Vernon recommends the construction of empirical SCP-based models for particular industries.[9] A proposed market definition model explicitly considers market conduct and performance relationships in technology-driven markets.[10] As Figure 7.1 depicts, the three market conduct variables are: (1) marketing orientation, (2) technological orientation, and (3) market definition criteria. The market performance element is market definition success. Success was conceptualized as marketers' perceptions of how well they understand and evaluate market definition determinants (i.e., customer groups, customer functions, and technologies).

Research Hypotheses

Based on the market definition model, six SCP-derived hypotheses were developed. The first three consider market conduct and

FIGURE 7.1. SCP Market Definition Model

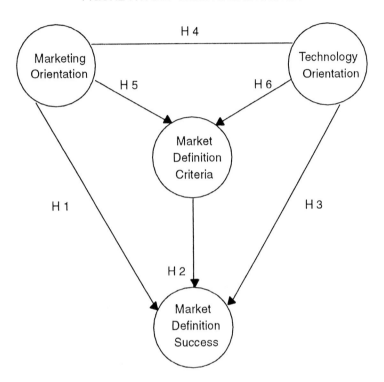

performance variables; the second triad examine market conduct-based relationships. A brief discussion that provides conceptual support for these research issues follows.

Market-oriented firms successfully implement the marketing concept (review Chapter 2 discussion). These companies mesh a customer focus with a competitive orientation by involving all people and functions in marketing programs and processes to accomplish organizational objectives. In the late 1980s Conner Peripherals, a new company (founded by Seagate Technology employees), quickly became the market leader in the manufacturing of 3.5-inch disk drives, a product ideally suited to the emerging portable computer market. Conner courted and won over Compaq (its key customer) and then flew past Seagate in a rapidly changing market arena. Seagate, the pioneer and leader in 5.25-inch drives, stubbornly held on to its core IBM-PC product, and they paid dearly for this strategic marketing blunder.[11]

Kohli and Jaworski propose that the greater the market orientation of an organization, the higher its business performance.[12] Narver and Slater's research suggests that market orientation and performance are strongly related.[13] Hence, the benefits of being market driven (customer oriented and competitor centered) is a truism for today's managers. Yet, in a recent study, only 15 percent of a multinational sample of large businesses qualified as being truly market driven.[14]

Day and Shocker explain that market definition criteria are important in defining markets.[15] The authors acknowledge, however, that their supply/demand perspective is simplistic and inadequate. Problems include the lack of suitability in many market situations, neither perspective is independent of the other, and there is little evidence that these criteria help management make better marketing decisions. Given these shortcomings, it is readily apparent that new criteria for effective market definition are needed. Based on a review of relevant literature, effective market definition is predicated on four main criteria.[16] Market definitions should be *multidimensional, flexible, operational,* and *future-directed.* These terms are operationalized as follows:

1. *Multidimensional*—several simultaneous, interrelated factors are required to adequately define markets.
2. *Flexible*—since market definition is important at different levels within the firm, it must be appropriate and adaptable for top management (e.g., long-range strategic planning) and lower-level marketing management (e.g., tactical decisions).
3. *Operational*—the "acid test" of the value of the market definition is actionability or its ability to be used in designing improved marketing mixes (should not be too complex nor too basic).
4. *Future-directed*—markets are dynamic and change over time. Static market definitions can lead to myopic marketing decisions. Future-directed market definitions help marketers locate new business opportunities and hit elusive "moving targets."

Technological leadership is also a viable means to stay ahead of competitors in markets. According to the Battelle Technology Management Group, the top ten technologies for the year 2005 will be: gene mapping; super materials for communication, energy, and transit; compact energy sources; high-definition TV; handheld electronic devices; manufacturing smart systems; antiaging products; targeted medical treatments; hybrid-fuel vehicles; and "edutainment."[17] The implication for management is that companies need to assess if they are: *cutting edge* (marketing tomorrow's technology), *at the edge* (selling today's technology—note that they may or may not be innovating), or have *lost the edge* (they are still trying to push yesterday's technology).

Technology-oriented firms have the ability and desire to use their substantial technological basis (e.g., strong research and development programs, new or sophisticated technologies, technically trained personnel, investments in plant and equipment, etc.) to develop new products and innovate in the industry.[18] As the electronics and telecommunications industries demonstrate, new technologies can redefine mature, as well as embryonic, markets. This in turn relates to the need for corporate mission and vision statements that are sufficiently broad (general) and focused (specific).

Hewlett-Packard and Intel successfully build on their technological prowess and exploit related marketing opportunities. In technology-based markets, successful market definition is predicated on a dual foundation—solid marketing and technology. The alliance of both of these critical business functions is necessary. Successful firms tear down perceptual fences (e.g., product managers interact with engineers). Technology is a core market definition dimension. This suggests that a synergistic blend of marketing and technology is needed to adequately define markets.

Furthermore, it is expected that marketing-oriented firms recognize the value of using market definition criteria in defining markets. Technology-driven companies may also benefit from such guidelines. Hence, the impact of the proposed criteria on the two key business orientations—marketing and technology—is an important issue to assess. With this backdrop in place, the six SCP-derived research hypotheses tested in this chapter are listed in Figure 7.2.

FIGURE 7.2. The SCP Market Definition Research Hypotheses

H1: An increased emphasis on developing a marketing orientation by technology firms is positively related to success in market definition.

H2: An increased emphasis on developing market definitions that are multidimensional, flexible, operational, and future-directed by technology firms is positively related to success in market definitions.

H3: An increased emphasis on developing a technological orientation by technology firms is positively related to success in market definition.

H4: An increased emphasis on developing a marketing orientation by technology firms is positively related to an increased emphasis on developing a technological orientation.

H5: An increased emphasis on developing a marketing orientation by technology firms is positively related to the use of the market definition criteria (multidimensional, flexible, operational, and future-directed).

H6: An increased emphasis on developing a technological orientation by technology firms is positively related to the use of the market definition criteria (multidimensional, flexible, operational, and future-directed).

Computer Products is a South Florida manufacturer ($224 million revenues, 1996 estimate) of power conversion supplies for communications equipment customers. This company narrowed its market scope, increased its investment in R & D, used concurrent engineering to accelerate new product development, and slashed overhead and production expenses. The results of this multipronged strategy that emphasized marketing, technology, and cost control?—a threefold increase in net income over a two-year period.[19]

THE SCP MARKET DEFINITION FINDINGS

Using a causal modeling approach, the SCP-derived hypotheses—conduct and performance relationships—were analyzed through covariance structure analysis (via the LISREL approach).[20] The four-variable market definition model was built from eleven unique indicators (see Table 7.1). Marketing orientation consisted of two elements: (1) the marketing concept (customer focus, profitability, and company-wide effort) and (2) marketing activities (sales forecasting, market research, and target market selection). Other compo-

TABLE 7.1. Correlation Matrix for the Market Definition Data

	X1	X2	X3	X4	X5	X6	X7	X8	X9	Y1	Y2
X1	1.00										
X2	.07	1.00									
X3	.28	.13	1.00								
X4	-.03	-.10	.06	1.00							
X5	.12	.16	.15	.21	1.00						
X6	.32	.16	.21	-.13	.03	1.00					
X7	.28	.25	.31	.08	.13	.33	1.00				
X8	.25	.22	.25	.01	.27	.28	.21	1.00			
X9	.15	.14	.16	.05	.03	.35	.41	.27	1.00		
Y1	.71	.09	.27	.03	.11	.35	.31	.28	.12	1.00	
Y2	.45	.02	.17	.10	.03	.25	.23	.21	.17	.58	1.00

Legend:

X1	Marketing activities (MKTGACTS)
X2	Marketing concept (MKTGCPT)
X3	Management technology (MGTTECH)
X4	Product technology (PRODTECH)
X5	Process technology (PROCTECH)
X6	Operational (OPERATIONAL)
X7	Future-directed (FUTUREDIR)
X8	Multidimensional (MULTIDIM)
X9	Flexible (FLEXIBLE)
Y1	Perceived market definition success (MDSUCCESS)
Y2	Success index (SUCINDEX)

nents of the model included the four market definition criteria (multidimensional, flexible, operational, and future-directed); three technological components (product, process, and management), and two market definition success measures (perceived success and the success index).

Five of the six research hypotheses were supported—four at $p < .01$ and one at $p < .05$. Table 7.2 provides maximum likelihood (ML) estimates and associated standard errors, initial estimates, and t-values for the relevant variables.[21] A practical interpretation of these statistical findings is next presented. The research results are organized into two subsections: (1) market conduct and performance relationships, and (2) market conduct relationships.

TABLE 7.2. LISREL Estimates for the Research Hypotheses

Latent Variable	Marketing Orientation	Technology Orientation	Market Definition Criteria
Marketing Orientation	—		
Technology Orientation	phi1 (H4) .28/.07,.25 3.77 **	—	
Market Definition Criteria	phi2 (H5) .32/.08,.32 4.26 **	phi3 (H6) .21/.07,.22 2.87 **	—
Market Definition Success	gamma1 (H1) .65/.05,.67 12.17 **	gamma3 (H3) .06/.05,.01 1.16 ns	gamma2 (H2) .13/.05,.20 2.45 *

Notes:

1. The first line for each relationship identifies the causal path in the market definition model (i.e., gammas 1-3 or phis 1-3) and its respective hypothesis.
2. The second line provides the ML estimates, standard errors, and initial LISREL estimates for these parameters.
3. The third line notes the t-values (ML estimate/standard error) and statistical significance of the relationship, i.e, ** $p < .01$, * $p < .05$, or ns—not significant.

Market Conduct and Performance

This study indicates that a marketing orientation has penetrated U.S.-based industrial technology firms. The two hypothesized relationships among the marketing conduct and performance variables were statistically supported. This is summarized as follows:

H1. Marketing orientation → market definition success
(t = 12.17, p < .01)

H2. Market definition criteria → market definition success
(t = 2.45, p < .05)

Webster noted that companies have rediscovered marketing's role in business strategy.[22] Market definition and selection decisions are a major priority for firms practicing market-driven planning. In the market definition study, 64 percent of the respondents gave an above-average rating to "perceived market definition success" (greater than 3 on a 5-point scale). Similarly, the mean score of 380 (based on a 100 to 500 range) for a weighted success index showed that market definitions were largely perceived as successful.

Marketing orientation was operationalized through two core measures, the marketing concept and a set of marketing activities (i.e., sales forecasting, market research, and target marketing). The ability to effectively use marketing activities was largely responsible for market definition success. The correlation between MKTGACTS and MDSUCCESS was r = .71 (p < .01), and r = .45 (p < .01) between MKTGACTS and SUCINDEX.

A logical outcome of a strong commitment to marketing is the development of a systematic approach to defining markets. Three of the four market definition criteria proposed—operational, future-directed, and multidimensional—correlated with market definition success (r = .28 to .35, p < .01). Flexibility was not significant, r = .12.

Somewhat surprising was the relatively weak positive relationship between technological orientation and market definition success (t = 1.16 for H3). Popular belief states that high-tech firms are technology driven and that an engineering and production focus is an integral part of a firm's market success.[23] There are two reasons why technology may not be a strong predictor of market definition success. First is the managerial transition from entrepreneurial/product-oriented enterprises to customer-driven companies. Second is the maturation of many high-tech markets (e.g., computer hardware, electronics, etc.). In such market environments, technological differentiation may take a subservient position to marketing differentiation.

Market Conduct Relationships

As Table 7.2 reveals, correlations among the three exogenous (conduct) variables were all highly significant ($p < .01$). They were:

H4. Marketing orientation and technological orientation
  $t = 3.77$

H5. Marketing orientation and market definition criteria
  $t = 4.26$

H6. Technological orientation and market definition criteria
  $t = 2.87$

We can interpret these findings as follows. First, a technology-driven firm does not have to abandon its technological edge to become marketing driven. Pharmaceutical companies realize that R & D investment is its lifeblood and is responsible for future breakthrough products. In the United States, drug companies invest 9.8 percent of their sales in R & D, which is more than triple the average of industrial firms in general. In 1995, an eleven-industry survey of 144 companies found that this figure, overall, was 3.2 percent.[24] Microsoft and other computer software companies also believe strongly in the value of research and development. Over the five-year period from 1991 through 1995, Microsoft averaged an R & D/net revenues ratio of more than 13 percent annually.[25]

Second, the acceptance of market definition criteria by marketers can be useful in developing market-driven strategies. Many executives acknowledge that they are intuitively considering such issues as multidimensional, operational, and future-directed market definitions. Unlike the four Ps (product, price, promotion, and place), for example, such factors are not currently featured in the marketing management literature. Hence, future business leaders (e.g., today's MBA students) may not be exposed to this thinking.

Companies should formally adopt these criteria, however, in future market definition and selection decisions—for example, incorporate them into your annual marketing plans, further develop and quantify the terms from your corporate perspective, and so on. Since the set of market definition criteria exerts a positive influence on market definition success, firms not using such an approach may place themselves in disadvantageous competitive positions.

Third, the significance of the technological orientation/market definition criteria relationship is interesting. This suggests that such criteria extend beyond marketing conduct decisions. A technological orientation may result in multidimensional, flexible, operational, and future-directed market definitions, too. The parallelism of marketing and technological forces is intellectually appealing and lends further support for a set of criteria for effective market definition.

In sum, top-notch companies do not make an either-or choice (technology or marketing). Great companies such as General Electric, Hewlett-Packard, IBM, and Microsoft use both orientations to their fullest potential to create and sustain competitive advantages. How strong are your marketing and technology orientations? Redefinition Remedy 7 provides a rating sheet to assess the concepts discussed in this chapter.

A RESEARCH AGENDA

In this chapter, an exploratory study of macro market definition issues was developed and presented. While this empirical test was illuminating, the market definition model can be further refined and enhanced (e.g., add an operational/service capabilities variable) in subsequent investigations. The sample size should be greatly increased and replications are desirable. Specifically, cross-cultural studies and longitudinal efforts would be particularly valuable.

One might argue that marketing mix variables (market conduct components) or objective financial measures such as sales or profits (market performance components) should be evaluated. Furthermore, barriers to entry and competitive intensity (market structure components) were beyond the scope of this study. While such extensions are worthy, a single test can only probe parts of a total theory without compromising the integrity of the work.[26]

This study was explicitly designed to assess perceptions of organizational conduct and performance by top marketing executives. Strong support for a marketing orientation may not be shared by technical or financial counterparts. Engineers and product development specialists may perceive their companies as more technologically successful than marketers. Future studies can assess market definition from nonmarketers' perspectives, too.

Realize that a market is a lot more than just a theoretical concept; it is a key to successful business strategy. In time, market definition can be elevated to a status on par with widely accepted managerial marketing terminology such as the marketing concept, the product life cycle, and market segmentation. Without empirical support and sound theory, it is likely to remain an issue strictly for marketing scholars and practitioners to debate.

SUMMARY

In spite of its importance as the foundation for effective business strategy, research on market definition has been quite limited. This chapter introduced the SCP paradigm as a new way to study the market definition problem. The use of covariance structure analysis clarified relationships among marketing orientation, market definition criteria, technological orientation, and market definition success in business and technology markets. These findings were summarized and interpreted. In Part III of this book, a three-stage managerial framework for defining markets is presented, implications for marketing management are discussed, and lessons learned to date are reviewed.

REDEFINITION REMEDY 7:
MARKET DEFINITION PERCEPTIONS

Circle *your response* to each of the following statements:

A. *Marketing Orientation*

1. We are customer oriented.	agree	disagree	not sure
2. We focus on profits, not sales.	agree	disagree	not sure
3. Departments within our firm work together to achieve objectives.	agree	disagree	not sure
4. Our sales forecasting is on-target.	agree	disagree	not sure
5. Our market research is insightful.	agree	disagree	not sure
6. We use information to create strategies.	agree	disagree	not sure
7. Our target marketing strategy works.	agree	disagree	not sure
8. We analyze our competitors' moves.	agree	disagree	not sure
9. We act on our competitors' moves.	agree	disagree	not sure

B. *Market Definition Criteria*

10. Our market definitions are flexible (adaptable within the firm).	agree	disagree	not sure
11. Our market definitions are operational (useful for developing strategy).	agree	disagree	not sure
12. Our market definitions are future-directed (responsive to change).	agree	disagree	not sure
13. Our market definitions are multi-dimensional (several factors define markets).	agree	disagree	not sure

C. *Technology Orientation*

14. Our success is due to product technology (ideas embodied in the product).	agree	disagree	not sure
15. Our success is due to process technology (ideas embodied in the manufacturing).	agree	disagree	not sure

16. Our technological success is due   agree   disagree   not sure
    to management know-how.

D. *Market Definition Success*

17. We understand our markets.   agree   disagree   not sure
18. We carefully evaluate market   agree   disagree   not sure
    selection.
19. Our market definitions are   agree   disagree   not sure
    unique.
20. Our market definitions are   agree   disagree   not sure
    successful.

Management Challenge

- You should be able to briefly explain all of your *agree* statements. For example, "we are customer oriented since we respond to all service calls within one hour" or "our market definitions are future-directed because they are based on market trends from the latest syndicated research studies."
- What will it take to turn a *disagree* or *not sure* into an *agree* statement? Provide specifics for each of those cases.

PART III:
MARKET REDEFINITION:
FINDING STRATEGIC ADVANTAGE

Chapter 8

Defining Markets:
A Three-Stage Framework

It is now increasingly difficult to define precisely where an industry begins and ends.

—Gary Hamel

Our company is in the very high performance, real time image acquisition, processing, and storage market as well as a relatively new market—digital video disks.

—Vice President of Marketing and Sales,
computer software manufacturer

Would you buy a $500 computer? While it is not marketing a PC, per se, Oracle is betting that millions of people will invest in an information utility (appliance) to handle basic tasks such as e-mail, Web browsing, word processing, and contact/time management. Market redefinition often means changing the rules of the game, a strategy that innovators such as AutoNation USA, Micron Technology, United HealthCare, Worldcom, and Yahoo employ quite successfully.[1]

DEFINING YOUR MARKET

To own your market and customers, you must clearly understand the presegmented market in which your organization competes. This must occur prior to designing target market strategies. Often, working market definitions are too simplistic. For example, some companies define their markets solely by geographic area (the

Pacific Northwest), product (pumps and motors), industry (tele-communications), state of action (the frequent flyer), or state of mind (the "techie").

Richer, more comprehensive market definitions are desirable; a multidimensional view of the market is advocated. Recall that markets consist of a blending of competition, customer groups, customer needs and functions, products, and technologies.

Among other market nomenclature, Kotler comments that marketers are concerned with available, penetrated, potential, qualified, served, and total markets.[2] While this concept of submarkets is quite helpful from a planning and mangement perspective, the terminology is at times confusing. Furthermore, Hamel and Prahalad note that many unexploited market opportunities are found based on unserved customer types and unarticulated customer needs. Products such as automobile navigation systems, cell phones, fax machines, and satellite receivers were developed in the factory first rather than specifically requested by the marketplace.[3] Building on these ideas, a pragmatic market definition model consisting of three levels and nine components is developed and explained in this chapter (see Figure 8.1).

THE STRATEGIC MARKET DEFINITION FRAMEWORK

Level 1: The Relevant Market

As Figure 8.1 shows, the initial challenge is to adequately define the relevant market (4)—the market appropriate for an organization given its resources, objectives, and environment. Identifying the geographic market (1), the trade area an organization serves, is a relatively easy first step. This is accomplished by using market scope (e.g., local, regional, national, international, or global) and other geographic market measures (e.g., census classifications, standardized market areas such as Arbitron's Areas of Dominant Influence [ADIs], and customer density).

Convenience (e.g., location) is a major factor in determining bank patronage. Productivity, profitability, time management, and training are some key business areas affected by an analysis of branch markets. Yet, surprisingly, most banks have not taken the time to geographically define the market area that they expect each of their branches to serve.[4]

FIGURE 8.1. Strategic Market Definition Framework

Level I: The Relevant Market

Geographic (1)

Generic (3)

Relevant (4)

Product (2)

Level II: The "Defined" Market

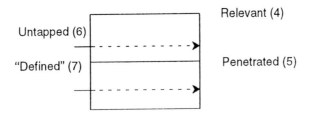

Relevant (4)

Untapped (6)

"Defined" (7)

Penetrated (5)

Level III: The Target Market

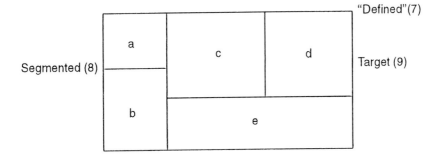

"Defined"(7)

Segmented (8)

a

c

d

b

e

Target (9)

Product market identification (2) is also relatively straightforward. Organizations can readily list the goods, services, and ideas they have available for sale. As an example, my consulting practice consists of the following services: training (seminars, speeches, and training programs on segmentation/niche marketing and market definition), research (segmentation studies, surveys, focus groups, and market profiles), and strategic consulting (marketing audits, marketing plans, market redefinition, target market strategy development, and visioning sessions).

Explicating the generic market (3) is a useful exercise to ensure that management is considering various and diverse marketing opportunities. While marketing myopia (narrow, product-oriented thinking) is avoided, a large market definition (typical of the generic market) may lead to a mass-marketing mentality and make a company's efforts and resources seem almost insignificant.

Defining the relevant market (4) provides a reality check for the organization; here a market definition is specified that is larger than the product market, but smaller than the generic market. The relevant market yields realistic boundaries to guide the management and marketing operations of your business. As an example, research found that the choice of a relevant market in the hospital services industry affects the technology adoption of electronic fetal monitors and centralized energy management systems.[5]

Sell-Soft competes in the sales automation (SA) industry. SA systems utilize computers to manage processes in the sales cycle from lead generation to postsale service functions. Sales automation products can be used for contact management, sales forecasting, service reports, integrated marketing management, and other applications. Sell-Soft's management can use Figure 8.2 to guide future business expansion strategies. Once the relevant market is established, we proceed to the next next stage in the market definition framework—the defined market.

Level 2: The Defined Market

Using the relevant market (4) as a departure point, we are now in position to fine-tune our market definition. The firm should assess its current customer base (penetrated market, 5) and noncustomers (untapped market, 6). Often the defined market (7) will include

FIGURE 8.2. Sell-Soft's Relevant Market*

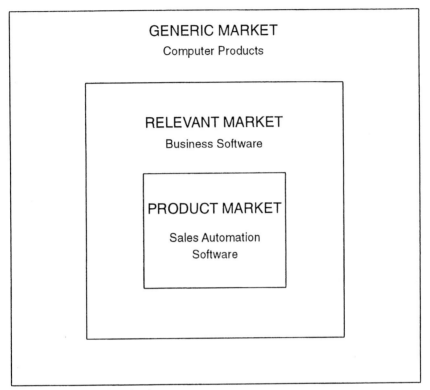

*Company name disguised

most of your current customers (although there are some customers that are not profitable to serve and you can afford to lose) as well as many new prospects.

Nypro, a plastics-injection company, took the market redefinition mandate quite seriously. As part of its corporate strategy to develop partnerships with a select number of large companies, Nypro phased out small customers. This plan reduced its customer base from 800 to 80! Half of the remaining accounts generated over $1 million in annual sales, with the other forty approaching that figure.[6]

Although Nypro's customer intimacy strategy made sense for them, do not think that you should say good-bye to 90 percent of your customers or just try to hit home runs (gain/retain million-dollar accounts). Rather, the willingness to occasionally walk away from "bad" customers is not a heretical view; it may be a sound strategy to allow your company to do a better job servicing solid, existing accounts and new, promising customers. For example, an electrical components manufacturer used strategic market analysis to win large-lot, price-sensitive buyers while selectively pricing itself out of a small-lot, specialty business that required overservicing. A revised, Level 2 market definition factors in annual growth rates, minimal acceptable sales thresholds, anticipated servicing levels, or other modifiers.

Level 3: The Target Markets

At Level 3, we take the presegmented market definition (7) and apply segmentation bases (e.g., geodemographics, benefits, usage, etc.) to identify groups of customers with similar characteristics or needs that are likely to exhibit similar purchase behavior; this is our segmented market (8). The specific target markets (9) selected to pursue with differentiated marketing strategies is the final element of the market definition model.

As an example, Winnebago learned that selling travel trailers (a new business venture that failed) was very different from selling motor homes (its core business). The customer groups are dissimilar, trailers are more price competitive, and they do not require service—motor homes do.[7]

MARKET DEFINITION APPLICATIONS BASED ON THE FRAMEWORK

Most small firms take a product-oriented rather than a customer-centered view of the market. Consider a company that says that it is in the emergency vehicle lighting business (product market).[8] This business competes in a tiny part of the aggregate lighting market (generic market) and in a small sector of the emergency lighting systems market (relevant market).

One prospective new product that management can consider is emergency lighting for mass transit. Since this initiative is located in the relevant market zone, it is likely that the firm will miss this potentially lucrative opportunity. This market myopia is caused by zeroing in on its current product market and ignoring new, but related business profit centers.

From a segmentation perspective, the emergency vehicle lighting market (product market) consists of ambulance, fire, police, tow truck, and utilities industries. Market size and competition will dictate which target markets or niches to pursue. As one ingredient in this business decision, the emergency vehicle lighting firm must realize that only about 500 fire trucks are produced per year, while approximately 100 times that number of police cars are manufactured annually.

As the previous example illustrates, not all of the nine market components play a critical role in every analysis. An integrated and systematic market definition process, as proposed, can help companies more effectively understand their customers, competitors, and changes in their environment. This knowledge means increased marketing performance. Table 8.1 provides a comparison of how two companies defined their markets based on the three-level market definition model. Redefinition Remedy 8 gives you an opportunity to strategize about your organization's relevant, defined, and target markets.

SUMMARY

A market consists of customers (actual and potential), needs, products, technologies, and competitors. One of the most difficult challenges managers face is how to define relevant and presegmented markets. A market definition too narrow limits potential opportunities; one too large leads to mass-marketing thinking and can make an organization's efforts and resources seem almost insignificant. This chapter reviewed useful market terminology and explained how a field-tested, multipart framework can be used for developing practical and optimal market definitions. Six management implications of market definition are discussed in the next chapter.

TABLE 8.1. Two Examples of Market Definition

Market Definition	Steel Company	CPA Firm
Geographic market	North America	Midwestern U.S.
Product market	Fabrication	Audit, tax services
Generic market	Sheared/bent plate	Financial services
Relevant market	Extra long and 50-foot sections	Business consulting
Penetrated market	Northeastern U.S. customers for construction equipment	Existing accounting clients
Untapped market	NAFTA steel users	Nonusers (clients and nonclients) of business consulting
Defined market	NAFTA construction equipment manufacturers	Growth-oriented, closely held businesses, new IPO companies
Segmented market	Cranes, concrete pumps, off-road construction, road construction	Businesses following a growth strategy
Target market(s)	Cranes	Sales growth >10% yearly, acquisition-minded companies

REDEFINITION REMEDY 8:
DEFINING YOUR MARKET—A THREE-STAGE APPROACH

Using the three-level, nine-part strategic market definition framework (see Figure 8.1), how might you define your market?

Market Terminology   Proposed Market Definition

1. Geographic
2. Product market
3. Generic market
4. Relevant market
5. Penetrated market
6. Untapped market
7. Defined market
8. Segmented market
9. Target market(s)

Management Challenge

• Schedule a day-long visioning session with the executive team to share with them your initial market view, solicit input on refining the various market definitions, disseminate this information to other managers and key employees, and develop strategies to best serve your target markets.

Chapter 9

Defining Markets:
Implications for Management

Our knowledge is a little island in a great ocean of nonknowledge.

—Isaac Bashevis Singer

It is difficult to find significance in market share calculations. Consequently, I've attempted to confine markets to the total number of dollars proposed in any business segment.

—Marketing Manager, computer manufacturer

Six key management implications regarding business market definition are discussed in this chapter (these are summarized in Figure 9.1). These strategic issues greatly impact the marketing performance of organizations.

FIGURE 9.1. Market Definition Implications

1. Effective market definition improves segmentation analysis.
2. Market definition provides a basis for marketing mix decisions (in particular, product management and promotional strategy).
3. Successful market definition in high-tech markets requires the development of a strong marketing orientation. The firm's technological orientation should not be neglected in this process.
4. Companies can use similar approaches or strategies to gain insight into how to define markets. Firms must tailor the market definition process to their particular situations, however.
5. Market definition decisions should recognize and respond to the increasing global nature of business.
6. Market definitions affect business expansion or consolidation strategies (i.e., potential mergers and acquisitions as well as divestitures of business units).

DEFINING AND SEGMENTING MARKETS

Market definition is the foundation upon which effective business/ marketing strategy decisions can be built. Unfortunately, many firms pay scant attention to market definition issues. These companies feel that they can clearly articulate their customers' needs and wants, understand competitive forces, and are "in touch" with market trends. Unconfirmed assumptions without the necessary fact-finding initiatives can be a prescription for disaster.

In the early 1990s, while others competed on price or frequent flyer programs, TWA introduced Comfort Class (the addition of three inches of legroom) as a new, valued feature for airline travelers. In spite of below-average performance in other service categories, TWA's customer satisfaction level soared to a leadership position based on J. D. Powers & Associates ratings. Hence, managers can change the game and creatively reshape the rules of their industry.[1]

To segment effectively, companies must precisely define the markets in which they compete. Segmentation means that markets should be partitioned by finding similarities in customer characteristics or customer purchase behavior. Dell's strategy of seeking sophisticated buyers and large accounts not requiring much "hand-holding" (i.e., limited technical support) is sound target marketing.

As Chapter 5 demonstrated, companies were heavily dependent on primary market segments that accounted for nearly 70 percent of their revenues. Hence, firms must devise marketing strategies to retain their existing customer base as well as find new markets. Although differentiation was the preferred strategy, and for the most part, a successful choice, a third of the sample pursued only a single market (split equally between undifferentiated/mass marketing and concentrated/focused marketing). The research showed that the latter strategy was clearly superior. For example, AirTouch Communications concentrates on global wireless communications (e.g., cellular, paging, and personal communication). Mass marketers are likely to benefit from a shift to concentrated target marketing.

The concept of levels of market definition (corporate, business, and program) means that STP marketing—segmentation, targeting, and positioning—can only be successfully developed and implemented if a definition of the presegmented market for the business unit exists. In other words, marketers cannot effectively utilize market segmentation analysis techniques (e.g., physical or behavioral dimensions) without a clear understanding and evaluation of the current market definition adopted by management.

BellSouth's recent reorganization from function (e.g., advertising, marketing, and repair departments) to customer operating units (consumer services, small business, large business, and interconnect) re-energized the company. This newfound service culture changed the way of doing business from emphasizing phone lines to meeting/exceeding customer expectations. Segmentation was conducted by demographics, lifestyle, needs, purchase history, receptivity to buy, and service offerings.

The dynamic nature of business and technology markets requires marketing executives to reassess (and redefine, as necessary) markets on a regular basis. The 3-D "plus two" approach—customer groups (market segments), customer functions (needs), technologies, competition, and products—offers a useful starting point for planning market definition and redefinition strategies.

MARKET DEFINITION GUIDES STRATEGY

The concept of the marketing mix (the four Ps) breaks down key marketing decisions into manageable subunits ripe for target marketing. While market definition may impact pricing and distribution decisions, it is particularly applicable to product management and promotional strategy.

Prahalad and Hamel use the metaphor of a large tree to describe a diversified corporation.[2] Using Canon as our example, core competencies are the root system—optics, imaging, and microprocessor controls. Laser printer engines are a core product, the trunk or major limb. Cameras, copiers, printers, and scanners are business units or branches. Finally, the Multipass C2500 is a multifunction, all-in-one product that provides color printing, copying, faxing, and scanning. This end product is a leaf or flower.

Market definition relates to product management—e.g., product introduction, evaluation, and positioning. Firms possessing these skills are cognizant of ongoing market and environmental forces. Givon explains that successful product policy means analyzing product weaknesses and strengths relative to competitive offerings and providing an adequate, but not extensive, product line.[3] This avoids the problem of product cannibalization. An understanding of the exact definition of product markets improves marketing decisions for new and established products.

Traditionally, the term *market* has been used in various ways; for example, take industrial pumps. There is the West Coast market, the product market of competitive offerings, the market of customers and potential buyers, etc. Dillon shuns these meanings and says that a market is a group of individuals who share common problems.[4]

Given this premise, the advertising function is the mass communication of a solution to a problem. AT&T's newest business strategy is moving from long-distance service to anytime, anywhere, any distance communications. This philosophy can be extended to integrated marketing communications programs, which includes customer databases. Similarly, this thinking can be adopted by regional sales managers since personal selling is generally the most important promotional strategy for key accounts in business markets (i.e., face-to-face problem solving).

Floppy diskettes, CD-ROMs, videos, or downloaded software can also offer excellent promotional opportunities for business marketers. Nordstram Valve's software assists buyers in selecting product attributes, understanding costs, and choosing custom-designed or standard valves. Premier Bank in Louisiania has found that informational diskettes helped build its small business loan business.[5] Companies opting for innovative media must be able to define their market effectively.

INTEGRATING MARKETING AND TECHNOLOGY

Technology can invent or redefine new markets. As an example, the multimedia industry had desktop PC-based publishing, consumer electronics, and broadcasting as its antecedents. The rise of the Internet has facilitated the growth of network-centric computing.[6] In changing and competitive markets, effective market definition is based on a strong marketing and technological emphasis. R & D activities and the marketing research department provide information and insight to guide product development.

In this research investigation, the acceptance of a marketing philosophy was strongly affirmed. Have managers overemphasized marketing at the expense of technology? The relatively weak relationship detected between technology and market definition success is an indication that technology has taken a back seat to marketing in many organizations. The implication of this finding is readily apparent. In many companies, senior management needs to rediscover technology, while maintaining its sharp marketing edge. Historically, Corning's "big-hit" strategy (lighting, ribbon machines, Pyrex, Corning Ware, fiberglass, etc.) has kept the company afloat.[7] A reassessment of personnel, decision-making authority, and the output of R & D logically follows.

Companies must meet a minimum threshold level for research and development (the quantity of the investment). How the funds are expended (the quality of the investment), however, is the real issue to address. Verespej stated that R & D investments by U.S. firms are often inadequate, excessive, or misdirected—geared to waning, not cutting-edge, technologies.[8] In contrast, Japanese firms such as Matsushita, NEC, and Sony do a better job of applying technology. Research showed that return on investment in R & D by small firms is five times that of medium-sized firms and twenty-one times that of large corporations.[9] This data lends strong support for companies such as 3M, GE, and IBM to practice intrapreneurship.

While market definition is largely a senior-level management decision, a joint decision making process is used by almost all organizations. Interfunctional input and the team approach to market definition is clearly advisable. Key players in this process should include marketers, engineers, and unbiased strategic managers (those with no allegiance to either the marketing or the technology camp).

A realistic appraisal of product, process (the ideas involved in the manufacturing), and management technologies (procedures associated with marketing the product and running the business) is also desirable. Consider these examples. Canon's superior product technology (cheaper, simpler, and more reliable than Xerox), coupled with its office supply retailer channel strategy, reshaped the low end of the copier market. Advances in process technology, via computer enhancements in the British gambling industry allowed patrons to place bets at the last possible moment. Philips' inability to commercialize its outstanding V2000 video system was an example of not capitalizing on management know-how; this meant delays, cost overruns, and ultimately, the Japanese succeeding with the VHS format.[10]

Based on my research, I found that small firms were more technology oriented than larger ones (which were somewhat more marketing oriented). In particular, small firms perceived themselves to be significantly stronger in product technology, while nonsmall companies fared better in manufacturing, the process dimension.[11] No significant differences were found with respect to management technology.

As companies grow, they are more likely to adopt and implement marketing practices. While this is commendable, they still need to think "small" and continue to stress technology. In summary, substantial commitments to both marketing and technology are recommended for effective market definition in high-technology markets. Companies such as AT&T, DuPont, Monsanto, Hewlett-Packard, Intel, and Xerox generally accomplish this dual objective.

This study also supports Dorfman's rejection of the Schumpeterian hypothesis.[12] Schumpeter claimed that large establishments are the powerful engines of technological progress due to their vast resources, risk-diversification strategies, and incentive to innovate in response to competitive pressures.[13] Others counter that small firms are more innovative because of their flexible organizational structures and risk-taking, entrepreneurial nature. Hence, there appears to be no optimal size; both small and large firms drive the wheels of technological advancement. Billion-dollar conglomerates and start-ups are equally vital to the future of technology-driven markets.

THE FIRM-SPECIFIC MARKET DEFINITION

As noted in Chapter 7, there are natural (industry) and enacted (firm-specific) market definitions. In this section, we are concerned with the latter, microperspective. How should companies ultimately construct a market definition based on dimensions such as customer groups, customer needs, products, and technologies? This complex question is difficult to answer; however, one word nicely captures what organizations must do to survive and thrive in the market-place—*differentiate!*

Sun's Java-based Internet strategy, which has generated accolades from software customers, complementors, and competitors, is how Scott McNealy and company shine brightly in a Microsoft-dominant universe. Differentiation means finding the strategic heartbeat or driving force of an organization (this is analogous to the strategic thrust concept discussed in Chapter 2). The strategic drivers chosen by an enterprise may come from one of ten areas: product/service, user/customer class, market type/category, production capacity/capability, technology/know-how, sales/marketing, distribution method, natural resources, size/growth, and return/profit.[14]

Darwin-influenced theory proposed by Henderson concluded that the business world operates very much like the animal kingdom.[15] Since no two species can coexist if they make their living in an identical way, business rivals cannot survive if they feature the same products and territory or attack the same customer base under the same conditions, using the same business strategy. Companies, similar to species, must evolve (adapt) or face extinction. The 5-D approach—customer needs, customer groups, technologies, products, and competition—offers a useful starting point for defining markets. Hence, a situation-specific rather than formularized approach is recommended. Managers must carefully assess all factors and their applicability to designing winning business strategies.

MARKET DEFINITION AND GLOBAL STRATEGY

Market definition decisions in business, service, and technology markets extend beyond domestic borders for virtually all organizations. Consider that the United States has about 5 percent of the world's population and 25 percent of the world's purchasing power. Can your company afford to give up 75 to 95 percent of the potential market?

Note that services are the fastest-growing sector of international business—they now account for more than 20 percent of world trade and 30 percent of American exports. The distinction between manufacturing and services has blurred in many industries such as health care. For example, Kodak now sells X-ray film and imaging products, but it also markets information management systems and imaging management systems.[16]

Strategic marketing planning should consider emerging international business opportunities. Regional market analysis is often the first step. Geographic market identification is relatively easy to conduct, low cost, and quite informative. The European Union and Latin America are frequently target areas of interest to U.S.-based multinational companies; Asia, Africa, and other regions should also be carefully investigated to find the best product-market fits.

Entrepreneurial firms not presently engaged in international business can consider altering their market definitions to include one or more foreign markets, resources permitting. Exporting is a viable market-entry strategy for the firm new to the international arena.

Forming international corporate linkages is also a recommended entry strategy for penetrating foreign markets or expanding overseas capabilities. Most high-tech companies are involved in dozens or more intra- and interindustry alliances—IBM has more than 20,000 such business arrangements.[17]

A greater understanding of how to define markets can be a competitive tool for U.S.-based high-tech firms to combat market share losses caused by Japanese and multinational companies. For example, consider the production of metal-oxide microchips—the fastest-growing segment in the semiconductor market. In 1978, seven of the top ten manufacturers were U.S.-based (the other three companies were Japanese). By 1989, this situation was reversed, with six of the top ten semiconductor companies Japanese, three American firms, and one Holland-based manufacturer. In just over a decade, this industry sector experienced more than a twentyfold increase in sales. Yet, leading U.S. firms saw their market share erode from 71 to 28 percent during this period.[18]

Rather than waiting for something to happen (e.g., an upturn in the economy, an improvement in the overseas business climate, etc.), firms should take charge of their own destiny through more effective international market definitions and marketing/business strategies. An interesting finding was that technology marketers in the sample perceive themselves as more globally-minded than they are in actuality. Sixty percent of the respondents said their firms do business outside of North America. Yet only 3 percent of the firms generated more than half their sales outside of the United States, and only 31 percent of the companies obtained more than 20 percent of their revenues from international markets. A more aggressive marketing program geared toward world markets is an opportunity available to many companies.

DIVEST, EXPAND, OR PRESERVE?

While most of our attention on market definition has been directed to the business unit, corporate views of the market are of substantial importance to the organization. Top executives must decide whether the company should maintain its existing configuration or alter its portfolio of businesses. The latter strategy may mean getting bigger (acquisitions or mergers) or smaller (divestitures).

In the 1970s, huge conglomerates such as ITT, of unrelated but profitable businesses, were born. In the 1980s, a merger mania that dismantled noncore businesses ran rampant . In the 1990s, restructuring is the operative word: mergers and spin-offs are both occurring in record numbers. A key difference is that today's deals tend to originate within single industries or closely related markets. The goal is to find measurable synergies.[19]

Streamlining

One researcher notes that the nineties could be dubbed the "era of deconglomeration" as a vast number of companies have divested businesses unrelated to their core competencies along product, market, and/or technology dimensions.[20] To get "lean and mean," a major focus of reinvention includes shedding business units not related to an organization's basic strengths or vision of future profit potential. Here are some examples illustrating the streamlining trend.

Xerox sold off several financial sevices businesses to concentrate on what it does best—digital publishing, color copying, and electronic printing. In the late 1980s, Cordis Corporation's sale of its huge, but troubled, pacemaking division reinvigorated the company. Today, this Johnson & Johnson subsidiary is the market leader in diagnostic angiography (cardiac catheters and related products) and has a strong market presence in interventional angiography (products that diagnose and treat vascular disease) and neurology products. Monsanto plans to spin off its slow-growing $3.7 billion chemicals business, which account for more than 40 percent of its revenues, to concentrate on its promising agricultural, biotechnology, and pharmaceutical products.[21]

Texas Instruments (TI) is literally betting the company on digital signal processor (DSP) chips. It is the market leader in DSP chips, which run cellular phones, fax machines, hard drives, modems, pagers, sound cards, and other products requiring high-speed, complex signal manipulation. TI has shed unrelated divisions such as defense electronics and portable computing and is acquiring DSP software firms.[22]

Other examples of companies that were recently involved in spin-offs include Bally, Sprint, Tenneco, Viacom, and even ITT. Of course, the most talked-about corporate reorganization has been the AT&T trivestiture (AT&T, Lucent Technologies, and NCR). While the jury is still out on this breakup, this bold strategic initiative seems to have provided these companies with much-needed market focus in light of ever-increasing competitive environments.

Mergers and Acquisitions

In 1996, announced acquisitions exceeded $1 trillion globally; and industry experts predict that the merger and acquisition binge will continue for the next few years or longer.[23] Some of the more intriguing merger initiatives have included Boeing and McDonnell Douglas, British Telecom and MCI, and Chemical Bank and Chase Manhattan.

While the Boeing-McDonnell Douglas marriage greatly increases market concentration in the aircraft industry, its global geographic scope, competition with the European consortium Airbus Industrie, and the reshaping of the defense industry has not presented major antitrust concerns to the Federal Trade Commission. This is in contrast to the FTC's close scrutiny in the blocked Staples-Office Depot, Rite Aid-Revco, and Microsoft-Quicken merger/acquisition attempts.

Computer Associates has grown to become the third largest software firm, behind Microsoft and Oracle, by acquiring dozens of small software companies. And Johnson & Johnson completed thirty-two mergers and acquisitions between 1990 and 1996 (the company prefers internal growth, but will selectively use acquisitions to strengthen strategic interests or gain important new technologies).[24]

Corporate Market Definitions:
Strategic Considerations

As our previous sections indicated, companies may try to shrink or grow to improve their strategic position in the marketplace. Rethinking the market/business strategy does not necessarily mean that a major organizational overhaul is required. Often, better market definitions are close at hand by following the principles espoused in this book.

Companies large and small must constantly evaluate the scope of their business to find their best fit in the market. In many cases, strategic alliances or joint ventures are superior strategies to mergers. In 1992, only 20 percent of U.S. CEOs viewed alliances positively; in 1997, 60 percent of these CEOs were favorably predisposed toward this market expansion approach.[25]

Managed care organizations and pharmacy benefit management companies have become an important force in the health care market. Vendors are now developing strategic alliances, sophisticated databases, and regional business units to stay close to their customers.[26]

Within organizations, different definitions of the market may need to be adopted for different business units or product lines. As an example, research found that the market for banking services varied considerably—hence, a definition of a product as all banking services is too broad. Small six-month certificates of deposits (less than $100,000) were found to compete in a national market, while Money Market Deposit Accounts and Super-NOW accounts compete in local or regional markets.[27]

The overall implication of this section on business divestiture, expansion, or preservation is that senior managers must carefully evaluate their portfolio of businesses. Are they the right ones for the organization or are some major transformations called for? In many cases, market definitions just need fine-tuning (see the seven-step process offered in Chapter 10).

DEFINING MARKETS:
OTHER STRATEGIC IMPLICATIONS

While the six management implications reviewed are of paramount importance, executives should also ensure that their defined markets accomplish specific organizational objectives. They should:

- be consistent with the business mission and vision;
- assist the organization in becoming more market focused;
- offer a sustainable competitive advantage;
- provide useful information to analyze markets (e.g., determine market position, assess market share, track trends, etc.);
- guide expansion decisions—geographic, market, and product; and
- help create a value proposition—this consists of a blend of product quality, service, pricing, and image attributes.

The premise of this book is that *visionary companies build markets today to become market leaders tomorrow.* Our final Redefinition Remedy, number 9, ties the discussion together by providing a blueprint for achieving market success; this, of course, is our ultimate strategic objective.

SUMMARY

Defining markets lays the groundwork for successful business strategy. In this chapter, we reviewed the major management implications of market definition. These were the market definition and segmentation link, designing product and promotional strategies, committing to both marketing and technology, differentiating to find unique market definitions, competing in the global marketplace, and organizational restructuring of business units. In addition, strategic marketing planning must relate to how management defines its market. In the next chapter, the market definition process is explained, lessons learned about market definition are recapped, and the concept of a market is clarified.

REDEFINITION REMEDY 9:
DEFINING MARKETS—A CHECKLIST
FOR MANAGEMENT

This exercise is integrative in nature—it builds on the eight previous Redefinition Remedies (RR). Al Ries, Jack Trout, and others have said that marketing is warfare. Used effectively, market definition and redefinition techniques offer management a powerful strategic, competitive weapon. Market definition blunders, however, can be the death knell of an organization. Here is an opportunity to test your business knowledge on defining markets.

RR1. Do you know what business you are really in?
RR2. Have you devised the initial market definition?
RR3. Did you use the 3-D and 5-D approaches to define markets?
RR4. Do you have a good handle on customer and competitive market definitions?
RR5. Are you using the appropriate business segmentation dimensions?
RR6. Have you carefully evaluated market redefinition frequency, motivations, strategies, and business performance?
RR7. How does your company compare to others in its industry with respect to marketing orientation, market definition criteria, technology orientation, and market definition success?
RR8. Do you clearly understand your relevant, defined, and target markets?

Management Challenge

- Are your key business decisions based on how your organization defines its markets?
- Reviewing the Redefinition Remedy summary statements (and actual examples, where necessary), identify your firm's strengths, weaknesses, immediate priorities, and longer-term market definition needs.

Chapter 10

Market Definition and Redefinition: Reprise

The market is not a place, a thing, or a collective entity. The market is a process.

—Ludwig von Mises

We manage markets, not factories.

—David Cote, CEO, GE Appliances

In this chapter, we review three major themes: the market definition planning process, lessons learned (insights and strategies for management), and the concept of a market.

THE MARKET DEFINITION PROCESS

As introduced in Chapter 1, companies can effectively strategically define or redefine markets by using the following seven-step method.[1]

1. *Assess the impact of competition and market uncontrollables.* Firms should choose appropriate approaches to compete in business markets (e.g., industry, industry segments, strategic groups, product markets, etc.). Market analysis requires an in-depth study of the competitive, demographic, economic, regulatory, sociocultural, and technological environments and associated emerging trends. Kodak's digital imaging business (annual revenues of about $1.5 billion) offers vast potential if the company can overcome strong competition from Hewlett-Packard and dozens of technology-led entrepreneurial companies.[2]

2. *Instill a strong marketing and technological orientation within the firm.* Internal market definitions (e.g., corporate, division, strategic business unit, product line, etc.) should be specified to take advantage of the organization's strengths in product, process, and management technology, while minimizing its weaknesses. The key is to excel in both marketing and technology. 3M lives and breathes entrepreneurial change. A new product "hit" culture permeates the company from the labs to the field sales force.

3. *Select the right mix of market definition characteristics.* Blending the proper degrees of customer needs, customer groups, technologies, competition, and products (the 5-D model) is the market redefinition mandate for management. Review the market definition maps and examples discussed in Chapter 3. This strategic task is necessary because firms have different objectives, resources, degrees of uncertainty, and situational environments.

4. *Utilize market definition criteria.* Operational (useful for strategy), future-directed, and multidimensional market definitions are particularly desirable. Flexibility (adaptability within the organization) can also be used, when appropriate. Market definition criteria exert a positive influence on corporate performance. Intel is an example of a company that passes this test. Firms should formalize these criteria in market decision making (e.g., market selection, strategic marketing planning, new product development, etc.) to gain a competitive advantage.

5. *Review and revise (if necessary) present market definitions.* In response to changing market conditions, the seven market redefinition strategies (and the no-change option) should be periodically analyzed for their effectiveness and efficiency. MAI Systems' struggle with the market redefinition process in the early 1990s is summarized in Figure 10.1.

6. *Implement and control new market definitions.* Marketing (e.g., product, promotion, pricing, distribution, etc.) and business strategies may need to be modified to best meet customer needs. As part of its corporate restructuring, Ryder System divested its well-known yellow rental truck business. The company sees its future as integrated logistics—coordinating distribution for commercial businesses.

7. *Look to other companies/industries for market insight.* Firms can also turn to other markets for insight and strategic direction. As an example, the automation industry has profited from lessons learned by computer firms. Although robotics lags behind computers in the product life cycle, other similarities exist. These include customer needs (labor-saving capabilities), customer groups (industrial/vertical markets), and technologies (advancement of equipment over time).

In the service sector, hospitals have benefited from marketing practices adopted from hotels. Both industries are highly labor-intensive, use bed occupancy as a performance indicator, and rely on intermediaries—travel agents or physicians—to generate a large share of their business.[3]

FIGURE 10.1. MAI Systems Corporation—A Market Redefinition Example*

MAI Systems, headquartered in Irvine, California, is a solution provider for the hospitality, process manufacturing, and gaming markets. In 1990, the company had 23 U.S. sales offices; employed 2,800 people worldwide; and had revenues of $400 million. As a minicomputer manufacturer, MAI competed globally with Digital Equipment Corporation, Hewlett-Packard, IBM, NCR, and others. MAI partnered with software houses using software as a giveaway to sell hardware.

Then the business changed. Microcomputers and networks cut into their market. Their giant rivals reduced hardware prices and offered total solutions. New competitive strategies were imperative. Management determined that they were too small to compete in this evolving marketplace. Plan A was to buy a competitor to get bigger. So they went after Prime Computers—a manufacturer with similar products and a similar customer base. But there was one major problem: Prime did not want to be bought. In response, they launched an anti-MAI campaign. A "white knight" came in and rescued Prime. MAI lost the takeover battle and $40 million in the attempt.

Plan B was to represent other companies as a Value Added Reseller (VAR). This relatively new idea sounded good to management. Why worry about production when you can capitalize on your talented (and well-paid) sales force? On a Friday, MAI's executives issued a memo that said that effective

---

*Contributed by George Matyjewicz, Managing Partner of GAP Enterprises, Ltd., Rutherford, New Jersey. Mr. Matyjewicz was formerly the National Marketing Manager at MAI Systems Corporation.

Monday they would be a VAR and the company would be segregated into seven business units. They purchased software companies who sold point-of-sale packages to retailers; textile software for dye houses; and programs for furniture stores, retail back office, lumberyards, manufacturing, medical practices, etc. There appeared to be no logical plan for these acquisitions.

Companies buy from a VAR mainly due to price. MAI's integration fee made them less cost competitive. In fact, in the first year following the transformation, for every dollar the company generated in revenue, they expended 99¢ on payroll! As an example, ten support people might be assigned to $75,000 deals. Action was necessary. Soon, budgets were revised, procedures and standards established, selling prices adjusted, and excess people were eliminated.

The market was also reidentified—from small companies to those with annual sales between $7 million and $70 million. Larger accounts (over $70 million) were handled by MAI's partners and their key account sales teams. Average sales skyrocketed from $72,000 to $325,000. Two major deals following the reorganization exceeded $1 million (previously the largest sale was $650,000).

While these results were impressive, other problems threatened the well being of the company. For example, MAI maintained a production group with a highly paid vice president even though they no longer manufactured products. Overall, corporate overhead was bloated; VARs should be lean and mean.

How should MAI have proceeded with respect to market redefinition? Here are a few suggestions: define the market; use a consulting firm that is familiar with VARs; hire people who understand the software market and know how to manage a software business; research market needs; and carefully analyze expenses, the value of time, and what it costs to support an installation.

DEFINING MARKETS: LESSONS LEARNED

The following section summarizes eight important market definition findings discussed throughout the book.

1. *Market orientation is more than hype*—this philosophy clearly improves the business performance of an organization. Market-oriented firms practice the marketing concept (customer focus, interfunctional coordination, profit rather than sales-driven) and are effective market researchers, strategic planners, and target marketers. These companies know their markets, cope well with change, and are likely to succeed in the long term. Consider two examples of market redefinition in the transportation industry. The ocean cruise industry repositioned itself from "the only way to cross the seas" to elitist vacation-

ing to a family vacation experience (floating hotels). Some old freight and passenger railroads reinvented themselves to become entertainment rides or sightseeing vehicles.

2. *Customer needs was the most important market definition characteristic* for organizations (twice as important as any other single factor). Customer desires and buying motives may vary widely within markets. In technology markets it is often difficult to accurately evaluate needs until after products are introduced. The transformation in focus from photocopiers (products) to document management (needs) revitalized Xerox in the 1990s.

3. *Competition is related to how markets are defined.* A narrow/ unique market definition can help find market gaps (untapped opportunities) in niche markets. In less than two years, Juno Online Services has become the second largest electronic mail provider (behind America Online) by offering free e-mail to subscribers willing to be bombarded with on-line advertising. Based on an international survey of marketers, it is predicted that industry consolidations will lead to fewer but stronger rivals and increased global competition in all key sectors of the economy (e.g., high-tech, industrial, and services).[4]

4. *The relevant market is the key market definition* within the organization. This is the market appropriate for an organization given its competitive situation, objectives, capabilities, and resources. This means that AT&T is in the communications/connectability business (not just lines and telephones); Baxter International provides patient healing and comfort (this extends beyond drugs and medical equipment); and Ciba Geigy's mission is not crop chemicals, but rather safe crop protection.[5]

5. *Technology creates not just products, but entirely new markets.* Technological leadership alone is insufficient for market success. Therefore, management must have a strong commitment to both marketing and technology. Netscape's bold Internet market penetration strategy (free download trials) catapulted its Web browser into the market leadership position.

6. *Market definition and segmentation are closely linked.* Target marketers (i.e., using concentrated and differentiated strategies)

were more successful than undifferentiated marketers. Segmentation success is dependent on a solid definition of the presegmented market. Dataquest found that PC and printer owners could be segmented by buyer's level of experience and attitudes toward technology. Innovators are likely to be upgraders, while technophobes generally are nonbuyers. A three-stage, nine-component framework can be utilized to define and find your market (review Chapter 8).

7. *Management should examine both natural (macro) and enacted (micro) market definitions.* Macromarket views explicitly consider the set of relevant competitors within designated geographic product markets. Micromarket views are unique and firm-specific; they may lead to customer/market ownership. Republic Industries has been gobbling up automobile dealerships and car rental firms at a frantic pace to consolidate a once-fragmented industry. Republic's co-CEO, Wayne Huizenga, was previously successful with a similar strategy at Waste Management and Blockbuster Entertainment.

8. *Market redefinition must be a top priority for management.* As called for, various redefinition strategies are available to management. Reassessing customer needs is generally the starting point. Customer groups, technology, products, and competition should also be carefully evaluated. Motivations for redefining markets may originate from the market or from within the organization. More than half of all reengineering efforts fail.[6] As the Cahners Publishing vignette demonstrates (see Figure 10.2), past success is by no means a guarantee of future success. Redefining markets can, however, be an effective response to coping with change. Business reinvention means listening to customers, using appropriate technology, clarifying the value proposition, and offering added value to the target markets.

THE CONCEPT OF A MARKET

Although the term *market* is central to marketing as a field of study and the basis of its origin, its meaning is somewhat obscured. A random review of five leading marketing textbooks revealed

FIGURE 10.2. Cahners Publishing—An Industry Leader's Market Erosion*

Cahners Publishing Company, a unit of Reed Elsevier, was the dominant business trade magazine publisher in the early 1990s. In its forty-five-year existence, Cahners grew to about 100 publications, 2,500 employees, and an average market share of 40 percent.

Initially, Cahners correctly viewed its market as business managers who needed management and technology information to effectively produce and sell goods and services. They first entered materials handling equipment and then most manufacturing, construction, and distribution markets. The company pioneered controlled circulation to reach more than 80 percent of buyers in a market and reinforced high readership with feature editorials on management practices and technology trends.

In the nineties, electronic sources gained prominence as a means for managers to access timely, detailed business information. Cahners' new executive team, consisting mainly of numbers-driven portfolio managers, largely ignored this vibrant trend and failed to listen to their editors, who were aware of this market shift. The Internet quickly reduced the value of Cahners' circulation files. Corporate downsizing eliminated many of the advertising managers and agency account reps that the ad sales team once called on; the clerk replacements preferred to do business by phone, fax, and e-mail.

The exploding computer hardware and software publishing markets soon became as large as Cahners' traditional manufacturing, construction, and distribution markets. But, the company had dated stories and did not provide the latest news and brand evaluations sought by readers. Hence, their market penetration was negligible. The management team did not understand the impact technology was having on distribution and how this diminished the role of advertising. While other publishers were rapidly developing Internet sites, Cahners was experimenting with CD-ROM versions of its industrial directories.

---

*Contributed by Jim Haughey, Adjunct Professor of Business Marketing, MBA Program, University of Massachusetts. Dr. Haughey was the Vice President of Market Research and Planning at Cahners from 1980 to 1994.

various definitions of a market.[7] Economists can add even more perspectives to the question "What is a market?" Perhaps, now is the time to revisit this idea. In an attempt to unify our thinking, an alternative definition of a market is proposed.

A market consists of people (buyers and sellers), purchases, need-satisfying products, and technological progress.

While the initial reaction to this new concept of a market has been quite favorable, it is recommended that further testing (and refinements) with marketing practitioners, professors, and students is needed. Ideally, marketing nomenclature taught in the classroom should be readily transferable to the business community. Realize that there are three advantages of this proposed definition. First, it is concise but comprehensive. Second, it captures the salient elements of other views of a market. For example, the core marketing concept of exchange (purchase) is integrated into this new and improved definition. And third, it reflects the key market definition (5-D) characteristics. To expand on this latter point, customer functions (need-satisfying), customer groups (buyers), competition (sellers), products, and technological progress (technology) are all represented. Progress intimates the nonstatic nature of markets—market dynamics tell us that change is the only constant in business.

Perhaps the ultimate example of an organization that has been able to react to its environment is Stora, a Swedish company that was born more than 700 years ago as a copper mining operation.[8] When threatened by Sweden's king in the fifteenth century, Stora evolved into a strong militaristic guild. Throughout the centuries, Stora reinvented itself from copper casting to forestry to iron smelting, and eventually to paper, wood pulp, and chemicals. How's that for redefining markets?

SUMMARY

Defining or redefining markets is an essential strategic decision for twenty-first century managers (for further evidence of this see the case studies in Part IV of the book). Unfortunately, there has been limited guidance for practitioners on how to find the right markets for their business units, companies, or products. Marketing scholars have offered bits and pieces of the puzzle.

This book attempts to give the complete picture. We have demonstrated that market definition is sound business judgment sprinkled with a dose of creativity. All of the marketing management basics must first be in place—e.g., a market-driven culture, clearly articulated mission and vision statements, strategic planning processes that work, customer and competitive research initiatives, targeted marketing programs, decisive leaders, outstanding people, adequate resources, and visionary executives that know how to project beyond "what is" to "what could be."

Defining business markets means assessing and acting upon all available market information. This knowledge base may be tapped from markets that are established, emerging, or even imagined. That is the market definition challenge! Are you prepared?

PART IV:
CASE STUDIES

Chapter 11

Market Definition Case Study 1:
The U.S. Newspaper Industry

Newspapers traditionally were a mass medium. While large general audiences remain the industry's core market, progressive newspaper publishers have realized the need for targeted sections, specialized publications, and nonprint products. Market-driven decisions based on information and feedback from the target markets (readers and advertisers) are critical for effective strategic planning in this dynamic business environment. A market profile of the newspaper industry is summarized in Figure 11.1.

Changing industry forces (e.g., competition, technology, consumer desires, and advertiser needs) required newspaper executives to reexamine the very nature of their business. This market redefinition meant that newspapers were no longer just in the "news business." The industry has been reshaped from a print media business for mass audiences to an information and entertainment services provider for targeted audiences.

The American newspaper industry in the late 1990s faces three major pressures that threaten its existence and future as a dominant media force. Specifically, newspaper executives must cope with market share erosion due to competing media and new technologies,

This case was written by Art Weinstein, PhD, Nova Southeastern University, Fort Lauderdale, FL. The ideas build on a presentation to the California Newspaper Publishers Association on February 9, 1995 titled "Segmentation and Niche Marketing in the Newspaper Industry." The author thanks Kathleen Newton, Publisher, Amador Newspapers, Jackson, CA, for valuable input and Marvin Nesbit, Florida International University, Miami, for research support.

FIGURE 11.1. U.S. Newspaper Industry Profile

Industry receipts: $46 billion

Total advertising revenues: $38 billion
    (retail 48 percent, classified 40 percent, national 12 percent)

Daily sales/readers: $36 million sales, 78 million readers

Sunday readership: 91 million readers

Daily/Sunday readership by age 18-34   46%/59%
                                35-44   59%/70%
                                45-54   65%/73%
                                55+   70%/75%

Daily newspaper Web sites: 500+

Top 10 newspapers based on average daily circulation (millions): *The Wall Street Journal* (1.84), *USA Today* (1.66, exclusive of bulk sales), *The New York Times* (1.11), *Los Angeles Times* (1.07), *The Washington Post* (.82), *New York Daily News* (.73), *Chicago Tribune* (.66), *Newsday*-New York (.56), *Houston Chronicle* (.55), and *San Francisco Chronicle* (.49).

Top 10 newspaper companies: Gannett Co., Knight-Ridder, Newhouse Newspapers, Times-Mirror Co., The New York Times Co., Dow Jones & Co., Thomson Newspapers, Tribune Co., Cox Enterprises, and Scripps-Howard.

Sources: Newspaper Association of America, 1997 (www.naa.org) and Audit Bureau of Circulation, 1997.

the struggle to maintain and attract new readers (e.g., the youth market), and the challenge of being responsive to demanding advertisers. Stephen Lacy, a journalism professor at Michigan State University, captures the essence of this recent market transformation:[1]

> The newspaper industry is undergoing structural change on a daily basis as a result of developments in communication technology and new patterns of media use by the public and advertisers. This process of adjustment requires new ideas for dealing with the problems that emerge from this change.

In an environment where change is ever present, successful newspaper publishers must invest in research, product development, and promotion to stay relevant with their two target markets—readers and advertisers. Such business initiatives are dictated, but unto themselves, they are inadequate. First, a new mind-set and marketing philosophy are mandated.

NEWSPAPERS AND INFORMATION PRODUCTS: AN EXPANDED MARKET DEFINITION

While daily newspapers remain the primary business for newspaper publishers (at least in the near future), the new market environment of the late 1990s calls for a variety of information-based niche products designed to appeal to specific market segments. Such specialized offerings include targeted newspaper sections/inserts, magazine-like supplements, audiotext services, fax services, on-line products, and other forms of information delivery. One industry observer offered an interesting perspective: "readers do not merely buy newspapers but solutions to individual problems."[2]

Hence, to combat declining readership and static advertising revenues, an expanded business/market definition is needed to find new revenue-producing opportunities. Robert J. Hively, president/CEO of The Knoxville (Tennessee) News-Sentinel Co., illustrates progressive 1990s thinking by stating:[3]

> Our philosophy is to be an information company, and an information company distributes information through newspapers, through fax papers, through campus newspapers, through zoned editions, through audiotext.

The traditional view and new view of the newspaper industry are depicted in Figure 11.2. As Part A shows, newspapers historically were product-oriented and served two prime markets—everyman (the reader) and general advertisers (the narrow arrow indicates that newspapers considered advertisers' needs to a lesser extent than their own).

The new market-oriented view indicated in Part B reveals that there are still two prime markets. However, companies must now

FIGURE 11.2. Newspapers and Information Products. (An Expanded Business/ Market Definition.)

Part A. Traditional View

Part B. New View

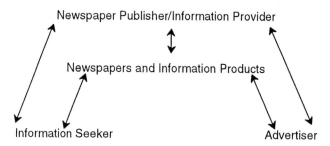

redesign the core product (newspapers) based on two-way input from diverse information seekers in a segmented market and focused advertisers trying to reach carefully targeted markets. *Interactivity and strategic partnerships* play a key role in the new era of newspaper publishing. Furthermore, just as Coca-Cola cannot satisfy everyone with its flagship brand, newspaper publishers must diversify their product lines to fulfill the needs of niche markets.

INFORMATION PRODUCTS REPRESENT NICHE OPPORTUNITIES

According to the Newspaper Association of America (NAA), newspapers still earn 90 percent of their profits from traditional sources.[4] While paper and ink will remain with us for many years, this statistic is declining annually. Aggressive newspaper publishers must search for new revenue streams to maintain and enhance their presence in highly competitive markets.

There are literally thousands of potential niche products available to entrepreneurial newspaper executives. Initially, companies should explore a limited number of niche concepts with the goal being to find one or two immediate winners; additional promising profit centers can be subsequently introduced based on the firm's resources, capabilities, and market position. Knight-Ridder, a newspaper conglomerate that publishes twenty-nine newspapers, utilizes different strategies in its various markets. Here are two examples:

1. The *Miami Herald*'s TeleHerald service offers more than 200 categories of information (business, sports, entertainment, and news) via a touch-tone phone.
2. The *San Jose Mercury News* is accessible electronically to more than two million subscribers of America Online.

Researching Newspaper/Information Product Niches

The ABCD rule for effective use of marketing means "Always Be Collecting Data."[5] A dozen low-cost research techniques useful for uncovering and exploiting newspaper and information market niches are detailed in Figure 11.3. Niches can be found in many places. A checklist of market opportunities for newspaper publishers/information providers is offered in Figure 11.4. This summary provides a springboard for developing a strategic market-based plan.

MARKET REDEFINITION: GUIDELINES FOR MANAGEMENT

The following seven-point program is designed to provide newspaper executives with a framework for coping with changing market forces.

1. *Listen to your customers.* As noted in Figure 11.3, information providers can benefit from a multitude of research techniques

to find their market. Consumers and advertisers need to be targets of this market intelligence effort.

2. *Involve the customer in the product.* As part of the interactive process and consumer-driven focus, contemporary newspapers/information products should be editorially relevant, reader-friendly, time-cognizant, and encourage user input and feedback.

3. *Test market, evaluate, and revise new niche concepts.* As shown in Figure 11.4, there are dozens of print and electronic niche opportunities. Qualitative (strategic) and quantitative (financial) screening criteria should be developed to assess new information products. Examples of the former set include, but are not limited to, the nature of the business preferred by top management and strategic synergy with existing operations, market trends, and level of competition. The latter group consists of sales and profit potential, return on investment/payback period, projected market size, and growth rates.

4. *Develop business partnerships.* Long-term commitments and/or joint ventures with compatible advertisers and other business service organizations (e.g., on-line information providers, sales/distribution companies, "competing" media, etc.) are the key to success in the age of relationship marketing. Value-added events, tie-ins, and co-op promotions are effective tactics for building mutually beneficial alliances.

5. *Invest in technology.* Information providers can use new technologies to expand their offerings and market coverage. While costly and still not perceived as a mainstream delivery option, recent developments in audiotext, databases, fax services, and on-line products have generated profits for scores of newspaper publishers, and their market presence is gaining daily. As part of Knight-Ridder's attempt to reinvent the twenty-first-century newspaper, the company tested a vertical Etch-A-Sketch-like electronic tablet—is this the next technological breakthrough?[6]

6. *Be unique/different.* Newspapers will remain a viable product for many years to come. Successful publishers are able to effectively differentiate their products from the pack. This is accomplished by providing substance and quality and responding to

market needs. The temptation for formula journalism and corporate conformance (be cognizant of the chain influence in the industry), however, is a potential threat to fulfilling newspapers' missions.

7. *Grow via planned change.* Information providers should seek careful, planned change, not radical transformation. Change means challenges and a reexamination of the basic operating assumptions for doing business. But, change also means great opportunities to those newspaper publishers/information companies that adapt and respond to new market environments.

FIGURE 11.3. How to Research Newspaper/Information Niches

1. *Secondary data*—use census data, statistical abstracts, Chambers of Commerce, *American Demographics* magazine, etc.

2. *Syndicated data*—purchase industry reports and demographic/lifestyle information.

3. *Do-it-yourself*—use in-house talent, assign project teams, work with consultants/small firms to supplement efforts, and conduct co-op research with other organizations.

4. *Ongoing customer panels*—implement bimonthly or quarterly sessions to gain insights from information seekers and advertisers.

5. *Low-cost surveys*—utilize telephone surveys, subscriber inserts, field intercepts, and piggyback research efforts.

6. *Qualitative research*—conduct focus groups and in-depth interviews.

7. *Input, suggestions, and complaints*—listen to the voice of the market; encourage calls, letters, faxes, and e-mail.

8. *College students*—tap these cheap but good services via marketing research courses, internships, advertising and journalism students, and Small Business Institute programs.

9. *Monitor the marketplace*—attend trade conventions, read trade journals, study competition and market forces.

10. *Concept tests/test marketing*—evaluate competing niche concepts, do small-scale rollouts of new products.

11. *Lead users*—find innovators with needs ahead of the general marketplace.

12. *Marketing information system*—create and use a database.

FIGURE 11.4. Newspaper Niche Opportunities

Marketing Implications	Niche Opportunities
Reader/information seeker:	
Demographic	Generation X products
age	
ethnic	Non-English language editions
gender	Information geared to working women, health issues
household composition	Single versus family life
Geographic	Regional editions
Psychographic	Sections based on readers' activities and interests
Usage	Variations in the frequency of information delivery
Advertiser:	
Relationship marketing	Joint promotions, long-term deals
Special promotions	Custom promotions, "advertorials"
Value-added services	Market research, targeted advertising
Technology-Driven:	
Database marketing	Customized and personalized papers/products, tailored advertising and promotions
Delivery/"packaging"	Fax service, on-line products
Interactivity	Telephonic and computer-based menu-driven products
New Products:	
Information services	Educational products/reprints
Research services	Business/market research, legal research
Total market coverage products	Nonsubscriber products (preprints, special publications), piggyback delivery

END-OF-CASE QUESTIONS

1. Market redefinition implies a change in at least one of the following dimensions: customer groups, needs, and technologies. In this case, it is apparent that all three dimensions have undergone dramatic change in the past decade. Comment on this.

2. The new market view of the industry is depicted in Part B of Figure 11.2. Explain the relationships among the three principals in this model: the newspaper publisher/information provider, advertiser, and reader/information seeker. How can advertisers use newspapers/information products to enhance their relationships with customers?

3. Describe how a small, independent newspaper publisher can use some of the marketing research techniques listed in Figure 11.3 to find market segments and niche opportunities (see Figure 11.4). Identify three viable niches and provide a rationale for your choices. How might your response differ if you were consulting for one of the "top ten" newspapers?

4. How should newspapers compete with other media in the year 2000? How should they define their business/market? What services/products should be offered and what market segments should be targeted?

Chapter 12

Market Definition Case Study 2: Sportmed

Sportmed,* a $100 million company, sells medical instruments and supplies to physicians who practice sports medicine—the treatment of sports-related injuries. This case illustrates how the company applies creative market definition to maximize customer and shareholder value and reinvent itself in a changing marketplace.

SPORTMED'S CUSTOMERS

Sportmed set the boundaries of its sports medicine instruments business area to be global in scope in order to encompass its customer base and its competitive threats. The customers for sports medicine instruments seek to satisfy the product needs of advanced features, multiple functions (the instruments can test for several injury or disease conditions), accuracy, and ease of use. Customers also seek to satisfy the nonproduct needs of ongoing education, service, reassurance through the company's image and reputation, and information provided through consultative selling.

Sportmed felt that all customers had the same broad set of four product needs and four nonproduct needs; however, the importance

---

* Sportmed is a real but disguised company. This case was prepared by Alan S. Cleland and Albert V. Bruno. It was extracted from their book *The Market Value Process: Bridging Customer and Shareholder Value* (San Francisco: Jossey-Bass Publishers, 1996). The scoring approach to market definition described in the case is part of the Market Value Process ™. For further information, contact Mr. Cleland at Cleland and Associates, Palo Alto, CA. This case has been reprinted with permission and adapted by Art Weinstein, PhD.

they attribute to those needs areas differ. For example, a young sports medicine physician may be just out of medical school and setting up her practice. She may be price sensitive because she has limited resources to invest. Due to her medical training, she may place great importance on advanced features and may value information provided via consultative selling. In contrast, an older sports medicine practitioner may be less price sensitive because he is well established in his field. He may be content with the current product offerings and see little advantage in the latest technology. Since his education is less current, he may value information updates through sales calls or ongoing educational programs.

SPORTMED'S MARKET DEFINITION

Markets can be defined based on customer groups (whose price, product, and nonproduct needs are being met), customer needs (what price, product, and nonproduct needs are being met), and technologies (how price, product, and nonproduct needs are being met). Customer groups are defined by age (young and older practitioners), and specialty—sports medicine specialists (SMS) and general practitioners (GP). Customer needs are defined by psychographics (progressives and traditionals), and patient diagnosis (muscle and tendon), and other. Technology is defined in terms of technologies for delivering results (computer display or printout) and the testing technologies employed (nonmicroprocessor-based versus microprocessor-based).

Although this discussion has been limited to two approaches in each category, there is no set limit to the number of approaches an organization should consider using to define its market most effectively. Sportmed's management ultimately felt that the specialty (customer groups), psychographics (customer needs), and testing technology (technology) approaches were the most promising choices for the three identified market definition dimensions. As Figure 12.1. shows, each Sportmed customer and potential customer can be assigned to one of eight potential market segments.

FIGURE 12.1. The Eight Sportmed Segments

1. Sports Medicine Practitioners/Progressives/Nonmicroprocessors
2. Sports Medicine Practitioners/Progressives/Microprocessors
3. Sports Medicine Practitioners/Traditionals/Nonmicroprocessors
4. Sports Medicine Practitioners/Traditionals/Microprocessors
5. General Practitioners/Progressives/Nonmicroprocessors
6. General Practitioners/Progressives/Microprocessors
7. General Practitioners/Traditionals/Nonmicroprocessors
8. General Practitioners/Traditionals/Microprocessors

EXTENDING THE MARKET DEFINITION ANALYSIS

Sportmed assigned all potential customers (its own and the competitors') into medical specialty and psychographic segments. Sports medicine specialists attached more importance to quality (product and nonproduct) than to price. Generalists, however, were considerably more price sensitive. Progressives were early adopters of new technology and willing to "pay up" for the competitive edge this equipment gave them in their medical practices. Traditionals were more cautious customers who waited to adopt new technology until it had been broadly accepted in the market; they were willing to forego possible competitive advantage in their medical practices and believed in "playing it safe."

A summary of the various weights by market segment and customer buying decision factors is summarized in Table 12.1. While both specialty and psychographics are useful discriminators of purchase likelihood, the psychographics approach is somewhat better based on total D-scores (60 versus 40).

Based on this analysis, Sportmed chose psychographics as the approach it would focus on in its initial market definition (note: management plans on repeating this process annually). Furthermore, progressives would be offered a line of high-end instruments reflecting the reality that quality factors accounted for nearly two-thirds of the buying decision. In contrast, traditionals would be targeted with a line of low-end instruments since price is the critical buying motivator (accounting for 65 percent of the decision).

Sportmed realized that whatever modest attention it gave to quality in the low-end market should emphasize product needs rather than nonproduct needs.

TABLE 12.1. Customer Buying Decision Assessments

	SMS	GP	D-Score	PROG	TRAD	D-Score
Price	40	60	20	35	65	30
Product	30	26	4	32.5	21	11.5
Non-Product	30	14	16	32.5	14	18.5
Total D-Score	N/A	N/A	40	N/A	N/A	60

Legend: SM—sports medicine specialists, GP—generalists,
PROG—progressives, TRAD—traditionals,
D-Score—differences by specialty or psychographics

STRATEGIC MARKETING CONSIDERATIONS

This simple but powerful first cut at a precision strategy for each market amply rewarded the effort Sportmed had invested in creative market definition by winning new customers. Sportmed's thirty-person top management group, including the president, divided itself into planning teams to build integrated customer value strategies in each of the markets it defined.

As an example, Sportmed devised the message, "Leading-edge software boosts diagnostic precision" as the foundation for its media campaign. This message nicely communicates features, accuracy, education, and consultative selling—important buying motivators to progressive practitioners. Ads in sports medicine journals, direct mail to prescription-writing physicians, and a trade show booth at a national sports medicine convention represented the heart of the promotional campaign.

END-OF-CASE QUESTIONS

1. Critique the market definition approach used by Sportmed. What improvements would you suggest to management based on the facts presented in this case? Should other factors besides price and quality be evaluated for the market segments?
2. Would you advise Sportmed to concentrate its marketing on the progressives? Why or why not?
3. What impact would cost factors, competition, perceived value, and market share likely have on Sportmed's market definition and marketing strategy?

PART V:
APPENDIXES

Appendix A

Sample Profile

Respondent Characteristics

Title	Percent	Count
President, CEO, etc.	29	58
Vice President	34	70
Midlevel Marketing	32	65
Nonmarketing	5	10

Gender

	Percent	Count
Male	88	176
Female	12	24

Education

	Percent	Count
Master's Business	31	62
Master's Nonbusiness	22	44
Bachelor's Business	19	38
Bachelor's Nonbusiness	21	42
No College Degree	7	14

Business Experience

	Mean
Years in Industry	15
Years in a Marketing Position	12
Years in Current Position	6

Business Unit Characteristics

Industry Classification	Percent	Count
Computer Software	27	54
Subassemblies and Components (electronics, semiconductors, etc.)	18	36

Industry Classification	Percent	Count
Computer Hardware	14	29
Automation/Robotics	12	25
Photonics (fiber optics/lasers)	11	23
Telecommunications	8	17
Medical, Pharmaceutical, and Biotechnology	8	17
Number of Employees		
< 25	30	61
25-99	28	56
100-499	25	51
$\geq$ 500	17	35
Sales Volume		
< \$10 million	54	110
$\geq$ \$10 million	46	93
Geographic Distribution		
California	20	41
CT, IL, MA, NJ, NY, OH, PA,TX	38	77
Other U.S. states	42	85

About the Sample

The random, multi-industry sample of U.S. marketing executives provides a high degree of external validity.[1] Sample participants included marketers from such companies as Bausch & Lomb, Harris Corporation, Honeywell, NCR, and Pfizer. The industries represented account for nearly 80 percent of the total number of high-tech companies in the United States, according to the *Corporate Technology Directory* (Corporate Technology Information Services, Woburn, MA).

An inspection of sample organizational demographics and population parameters showed no major differences based on three of the four important characteristics—industry classification, sales volume, and geographic distribution of the firms (number of employees was the exception). Hence, it can be concluded that the data were obtained from a representative sample of business units.

The findings in this study are also relevant for quasi high-tech industries such as advanced materials, chemicals, defense, transportation, etc. In addition, industrial firms and business service providers are likely to benefit from the insights gained. This was confirmed via focus groups conducted with eighteen marketing executives in Pittsburgh and Minneapolis and a small-scale, national pretest (n = 48) conducted prior to the quantitative survey.

Appendix B

Market Definition Survey

Part A: Present Market Definitions

1. *In your firm*, at what levels are markets defined? (Indicate frequency by circling your response.)

	Never	Sometimes	Often	Always
a. Corporate—overall company	1	2	3	4
b. Division—major part of firm (e.g., West Coast or instrumentation divisions)	1	2	3	4
c. Strategic business unit (SBU)—separate profit center within a division	1	2	3	4
d. Product line—set of closely related products	1	2	3	4
e. Product or brand	1	2	3	4

2. From *your* perspective, how are *competitive markets* defined? (Indicate frequency by circling your response.)

	Never	Sometimes	Often	Always
a. Corporate definition—cuts across two or more industries	1	2	3	4
b. Industry—a branch of trade (e.g., the computer industry)	1	2	3	4
c. Industry sector—part of an industry (e.g., microcomputers)	1	2	3	4

	Never	Sometimes	Often	Always
d. Strategic groups—a set of firms following similar competitive strategies	1	2	3	4
e. Generic market—potential customers with similar needs but differing ways of satisfying them (e.g., business communication)	1	2	3	4
f. Product market—potential customers with similar ways of satisfying needs (e.g., fax machines)	1	2	3	4
g. Standard Industrial Classification (SIC) codes	1	2	3	4

---

3. a. The level of management *primarily* responsible for market definition in *your firm* is:
   _____ Upper-Level _____ Middle-level _____ Lower-level
   b. The title of the person *primarily* responsible for market definition decisions in *your firm* is the: _____
   c. Is a joint decision process used in defining markets?
   _____ Yes   _____ No

---

4. Rate the following market definition characteristics based on their importance to *your firm*. Allocate *100* points among those characteristics most important to your firm. (For example, if you feel that competition, products, and technologies are most important, you might allocate 40, 35, and 25 points, respectively. Another option might be 4 factors all receiving 25 points. You may allocate points to as many or as few characteristics as you wish. There is no right or wrong response.)

   _____1. Competition
   _____2. Customer groups (market segments)
   _____3. Customer needs
   _____4. Environmental factors (economic, political, regulatory)

_____5. Geographic area
_____6. Market share
_____7. Products
_____8. Technologies

TOTAL = 100

---

5. Rate <u>your firm's</u> success in understanding and evaluating the market definition characteristics. (Circle your response for each.)

	(1) Unsuccessful	(2) Somewhat Unsuccessful	(3) Somewhat Successful	(4) Successful	(5) Very Successful
1. Competition	1	2	3	4	5
2. Customer groups	1	2	3	4	5
3. Customer needs	1	2	3	4	5
4. Environmental	1	2	3	4	5
5. Geographic area	1	2	3	4	5
6. Market share	1	2	3	4	5
7. Products	1	2	3	4	5
8. Technologies	1	2	3	4	5

---

6. Overall, how successful is *your firm* in the following marketing activities? (Circle your response for each.)

	(1) Unsuccessful	(2) Somewhat Unsuccessful	(3) Somewhat Successful	(4) Successful	(5) Very Successful
1. Sales forecasting	1	2	3	4	5
2. Market research	1	2	3	4	5
3. Target marketing	1	2	3	4	5
4. Understanding and evaluating markets	1	2	3	4	5

---

7. *Your firm's* market definitions can be characterized as: (Choose one.)

_____ Undifferentiated—one marketing program for all customer segments

_____ Focused—concentrate on a single customer segment
_____ Differentiated—multiple customer segments, separate
        marketing programs developed

Part B: Market Redefinition

1. a. How many times has *your firm* redefined its market during the
      past five years? _____ times
      (Note: a market redefinition means your firm pursued new target
      markets, appealed to new market needs, or changed technolo-
      gies.)
   b. When did *your firm* last redefine its market? _____
   c. What prompted this redefinition? Allocate *100* points to the
      following factors. (For example, if you feel that management
      decision and competition were equally important, you would
      allocate 50 points to each factor. You may allocate points to any
      or all factors.)
      _____1. Management decision
      _____2. Organizational/personnel change
      _____3. Sales below expectations
      _____4. Technology
      _____5. Acquisition/merger
      _____6. Competition
      _____7. Market analysis
      _____8. Industry regulation
      _____9. Other _____

TOTAL = 100

---

2. When *your firm* last redefined the market, did the company: (Circle
   your responses.)

   a. Change customer groups (market segments)?   Yes   No
   b. Change customer functions (appeal to new
      market needs)?   Yes   No
   c. Change technologies?   Yes   No

Part C: Market Definition Perceptions

1. On a 5-point scale, where "1" is strongly disagree, "2" is disagree,
   "3" is neither agree nor disagree, "4" is agree, and "5" is strongly
   agree, circle *your response* to each of the following statements:

	SD	D	N	A	SA
a. Our firm's market definitions are flexible (adaptable within the firm).	1	2	3	4	5
b. Our firm's market definitions are operational (useful for strategy).	1	2	3	4	5
c. Our firm's market definitions are future-directed (responsive to change).	1	2	3	4	5
d. Our firm's market definitions are multidimensional (several factors define markets).	1	2	3	4	5
e. Our firm's market definitions are successful.	1	2	3	4	5
f. Our firm's success is due to product technology (ideas embodied in the product).	1	2	3	4	5
g. Our firm's success is due to process technology (ideas embodied in manufacturing).	1	2	3	4	5
h. Our firm's technological success is due to management know-how	1	2	3	4	5
i. Our firm's success is due to overall technology.	1	2	3	4	5

2. Using the same five-point scale, respond to each of the following statements concerning *your competitive market:*

	SD	D	N	A	SA
a. Firms will be more customer oriented.	1	2	3	4	5
b. Firms will concentrate their efforts more on profits than sales volume.	1	2	3	4	5
c. Marketers will work together with other functional departments in the firm to achieve total company objectives.	1	2	3	4	5

	SD	D	N	A	SA
d. Firms will spend more on marketing due to increased competition.	1	2	3	4	5
e. Firms in our industry will aggressively fight to hold on to market share.	1	2	3	4	5
f. Competition will be more intense.	1	2	3	4	5

3. Please indicate *your* agreement/disagreement with the following two statements describing markets. Markets consist of:

	SD	D	N	A	SA
a. buyers and sellers and are defined by geography, product type, price uniformity, and product substitutability.	1	2	3	4	5
b. all potential customers sharing a particular need or want who might be willing and able to engage in exchange to satisfy that need or want.	1	2	3	4	5

Part D: Classification Information (Confidential)

1. Background information on your business/business unit

   a. Primary industry (please specify)   _____
   b. Geographic area served   _____
   c. Number of employees   _____
   d. Research and development (% of sales)   _____%

2. Financial information for your business/business unit

   a. Annual sales $_____
   b. Annual sales growth rate   _____%
   c. Annual sales growth rate, industry   _____%

d. % Revenues from international sales   _____%
e. % Sales from primary market segment   _____%
f. Market share in principal market   _____%

3. Respondent/personal information

a. Number of years in current job   _____
b. Number of years in this industry   _____
c. Number of years in a marketing position   _____
d. Undergraduate degree, major   _____
   Graduate degree, major   _____
e. Number of professional courses taken in   _____
   marketing (e.g., AMA, Burke, etc.)

4. Comments? (Please attach.)

THANKS FOR YOUR COOPERATION
AND ASSISTANCE!

Brief Note on Survey Validity and Reliability

External validity (generalizability) was demonstrated via the representative sample of marketing executives discussed in Appendix A. In addition, the study fared well with respect to content validity. The questionnaire clearly and comprehensively specified the domain (market definition) based on sound theory from marketing and related disciplines. Pretests and input from marketers integrated practitioner issues into the research instrument.

Most of the findings met a threefold test for validity—i.e., results are valid if they are statistically significant at the 95 percent level or better, conform to the best available theory, and make sense to the knowledgeable businessperson.[1] Correlation analyses help establish construct validity, based on strong theoretical support.[2] For the most part, significant correlations were evidenced between observables as predicted (e.g., marketing activities and market definition criteria with the market definition success indicators). Similarly, variables theorized as unrelated had nonsignificant correlations. Confirmatory factor analysis and factor analysis provided further insight on convergent and divergent validity and reliability.

Overall, the scales used in this study demonstrated modest reliabilities (coefficient alphas of about .70).[3] This is not surprising since most of these measures are new and evolving. Therefore, opportunities for improving these measures exist.

Notes

PART I: DEFINING BUSINESS MARKETS: A PRIMER

Chapter 1

1. Merck & Co., *Merck Annual Report,* Whitehouse Station, NJ: Merck & Co., 1995, inside front cover.
2. Walter S. Mossberg, "Now Apple Users Can Take Advantage of New Mac Clone," *The Wall Street Journal,* May 18, 1995, p. B1.
3. Ralf Boscheck, "Health Care Reform and the Restructuring of the Pharmaceutical Industry," *Long-Range Planning,* 29(5), 1996, pp. 629-642.
4. Robert D. Hof, "Where Did the Net Come from, Daddy?," *Business Week,* September 16, 1996, p. 19.
5. Erik G. Rule, "What's Happening to Strategic Planning in Canadian Businesses?," *Business Quarterly,* March 1987, pp. 43-47.
6. J. G. M. Curran and J. H. Goodfellow, "Theoretical and Practical Issues in the Determination of Market Boundaries," *European Journal of Marketing,* 24(1), 1990, pp. 16-28.
7. Michael Hammer and James Champy, *Reengineering the Corporation,* New York: Harper Business, 1993.
8. Alan Deutschman, "How HP Continues to Grow," *Fortune,* May 2, 1994, pp. 90-100.
9. Gary Hamel and C. K. Prahalad, *Competing for the Future,* Boston: Harvard Business School, 1994, p. 15.
10. Art Weinstein, "Market Definition: Strategies and Guidelines for Technology Executives," *Competitive Intelligence Review,* 6(3), 1995, pp. 55-56. Much of this section first appeared in this article.
11. Peter F. Drucker, *Management: Tasks, Responsibilities, and Practices,* New York: Harper & Row, 1974.

Chapter 2

1. Jack Sissors, "What Is a Market?," *Journal of Marketing,* 30, July 1966, pp. 17-21.
2. James H. Myers and Edward Tauber, *Market Structure Analysis,* Chicago: American Marketing Association, 1977.

3. Russell I. Haley, *Developing Effective Communications Strategies: A Benefit Segmentation Approach,* New York: John Wiley and Sons, pp. 94-109.

4. Many articles were written using market structure methodology in the late 1970s/early 1980s. Some of the more important works include: Jacques C. Bourgeois, George H. Haines, Jr., and Montrose S. Somers, "Defining an Industry," presented at Joint TIMS/ORSA Conference, Las Vegas, Nevada, 1975; George S. Day, Allen D. Shocker, and Rajendra K. Srivastava, "Customer-Oriented Approaches to Identifying Product-Markets," *Journal of Marketing,* 43, Fall 1979, pp. 8-19; and Rajendra K. Srivastava, Mark I. Albert, and Allan D. Shocker, "A Customer-Oriented Approach for Determining Market Structures," *Journal of Marketing,* 48, Spring 1984, pp. 32-45.

5. Gary L. Frazier and Roy D. Howell, "Business Definition and Performance," *Journal of Marketing,* 47, Spring 1983, pp. 59-67.

6. Robert Buzzell and Bradley T. Gale, *The PIMS Principles: Linking Strategy to Performance,* New York: The Free Press, 1987.

7. Derek F. Abell, *Defining the Business: The Starting Point of Strategic Planning,* Englewood Cliffs, NJ: Prentice-Hall, 1980.

8. Ibid.

9. Sandy Hock, "Jackson Hewitt Shops for Clients at 18 Wal-Marts," *Accounting Today,* October 1994, pp. 1-2.

10. David Poppe, "Accounting Profession Braces for Big Changes," *Miami Herald,* March 9, 1997, 1F, 7F.

11. Theodore Levitt, "Marketing Myopia," *Harvard Business Review,* July-August 1960, pp. 45-56.

12. Dhananjayan Kashyap, "Marketing Myopia Revisited: A View Through the 'Coloured' Looking Glass of a Client," *Marketing and Research Today,* August 1996, pp. 197-201.

13. Michael D. Richard, James A. Womack, and Arthur A. Allaway, "An Integrated View of Marketing Myopia," *Journal of Consumer Marketing,* 9, Summer 1992, pp. 65-71.

14. Michael Treacy and Fred Wiersema, *The Discipline of Market Leaders,* Reading, MA: Addison-Wesley, 1995.

15. Stanley F. Slater and John C. Narver, "Market Orientation, Customer Value, and Superior Performance," *Business Horizons,* March-April 1994, pp. 22-28.

16. Hilton Barrett, "Ultimate Goal Is to Anticipate the Needs of the Market," *Marketing News,* October 7, 1996, p. 4.

17. The two key articles that were springboards for subsequent research were: John C. Narver and Stanley F. Slater, "The Effect of a Market Orientation on Business Profitability," *Journal of Marketing,* 54, October 1990, pp. 20-35; and Ajay Kohli and Bernard J. Jaworski, "Market Orientation: The Construct, Research Propositions, and Managerial Implications," *Journal of Marketing,* 54, April 1990, pp. 1-18.

18. P. S. Raju, Subhas C. Lonial, and Yash P. Gupta, "Market Orientation and Performance in the Hospital Industry," *Journal of Health Care Marketing,* 15, Winter 1995, pp. 34-41.

19. Charles A. Rarick and John Vitton, "Mission Statements Make Cents," *Journal of Business Strategy,* 16, January-February 1995, pp. 11-12.

20. Romuald A. Stone, "Mission Statements Revisited," *SAM Advanced Management Journal,* 61, Winter 1996, pp. 31-37.

21. Patricia Jones and Larry Kahaner, *Say It and Live It: The 50 Corporate Mission Statements That Hit the Mark,* New York: Doubleday, 1995, pp. 135-139.

22. James C. Collins and Jerry I. Porras, "Building Your Company's Vision," *Harvard Business Review,* September-October 1996, pp. 65-77.

23. Joseph V. Quigley, "Vision: How Leaders Develop It, Share It, and Sustain It," *Business Horizons,* 37, September-October 1994, pp. 37-41.

24. Richard G. Hamermesh, *Fad-Free Management: The Six Principles That Drive Successful Companies and Their Leaders,* Santa Monica, CA: Knowledge Exchange, 1996.

25. Jeffrey Abrahams, *The Mission Statement Book,* Berkeley, CA: Ten Speed Press, 1995, pp. 162-163.

26. William A. Sherden, *Market Ownership: The Art & Science of Becoming #1,* New York: Amacom, 1994.

27. Sandra Vandermerwe, "Becoming a Customer-Owning Corporation," *Long-Range Planning,* 29(6), 1996, pp. 770-782.

PART II: MARKET DEFINITION: RESEARCH FINDINGS

Chapter 3

1. Derek F. Abell, *Defining the Business: The Starting Point of Strategic Planning,* Englewood Cliffs, NJ: Prentice-Hall, 1980.

2. Robert D. Buzzell, *Note on Market Definition and Segmentation,* Cambridge, MA: Harvard Business School, 1978.

3. Derek F. Abell, *Managing with Dual Strategies,* New York: Free Press, 1993.

4. Ron McTavish, "One More Time: What Business Are You In?," *Long-Range Planning,* 28(2), 1995, pp. 49-60.

5. Patricia Buckley and M. Daniel Westbrook, "Market Definition and Assessing the Competitive Relationship Between Rail and Truck Transportation," *Journal of Regional Science,* 31(3), 1991, pp. 329-346.

6. Briance Mascarenhas, "First-Mover Effects in Multiple Dynamic Markets," *Strategic Management Journal,* 13, 1992, pp. 237-243.

7. Andrew C. Hruska, "A Broad Market Approach to Antitrust Product Market Definition in Innovative Industries," *The Yale Law Journal,* 102, 1992, pp. 305-331.

8. Robert Pitofsky, "New Definitions of Relevant Market and the Assault on Antitrust," *Columbia Law Review,* 90(7), pp. 1805-1864.

9. Production/distribution was not considered as important in two focus groups. Hence, this factor was not tested in the quantitative survey.

10. John A. Martilla and John C. James, "Importance-Performance Analysis," *Journal of Marketing,* 41, January 1977, pp. 77-79.

11. Lee Graf, Masoud Hemmasi, and Kelly C. Strong, "Strategic Analysis for Resource Allocation Decisions in Health Care Organizations," *Journal of Managerial Issues,* 8, Spring 1996, pp. 92-107.

12. These results were first reported in Art Weinstein, "Market Definition and Redefinition: An Application to Industrial High-Tech Markets," in David W. Stewart and Naufel J. Vilcassem (Eds.), *American Marketing Association Winter Educators' Conference Proceedings,* La Jolla, CA, 1995, pp. 277-284.

13. Genevieve Capowski, "The Force of Value," *Management Review,* May 1995, pp. 33-38.

14. Anne Moncrieff Arrate, "What, Not Where, Rules the Day at PR Agency," *Miami Herald Business Monday,* November 27, 1995, p. 21.

15. BellSouth Corporation, *BellSouth Annual Report,* Atlanta: BellSouth Corporation, 1996, p. 28.

Chapter 4

1. Subhash C. Jain, *Marketing Planning and Strategy,* Third Edition, Cincinnati: Southwestern Publishing Co., 1990.

2. David Kirkpatrick, "They're All Copying Compaq," *Fortune,* November 25, 1996, pp. 28, 32.

3. David B. Francis, "Your Competitors: Who Will They Be?," in Jennifer Swanson (Ed.), *Society of Competitive Intelligence Professionals Annual Conference Proceedings,* March 27-30, 1996, pp. 336-348.

4. Cindy Krischer Goodman, "Law Giant Opens New Consulting Division," *Miami Herald,* February 27, 1997, pp. C1, 3.

5. George S. Day, "Strategic Market Analysis and Definition: An Integrated Approach," *Strategic Management Journal,* 2, May 1981, pp. 281-299.

6. These findings first published in Art Weinstein, "Market Definition in Technology-Based Industry: A Comparative Study of Small Versus Non-Small Companies," *Journal of Small Business Management,* October 1994, pp. 28-36.

7. The transformation of the banking industry is nicely captured in Alexandra Clough, "They're All After Your Money," *Florida Trend,* October 1995, pp. 66-73.

8. Saul W. Gellerman and Robert J. Potter, "The Ultimate Strategic Question," *Business Horizons,* March-April 1996, pp. 5-10.

9. Gary R. Trugman, "Must Small Firms Specialize to Survive? Yes," *Journal of Accountancy,* January 1995, pp. 41-43.

10. G. Easton, "Competition and Marketing Strategy," *European Journal of Marketing,* 22(2), 1987, pp. 31-49.

11. Kristin Dunlap Godsey, "Hit the Ground Running," *Success,* December 1996, pp. 36-44.

12. Anthony E. Boardman and Aidan R. Vining, "Defining Your Business Using Product-Customer Matrices," *Long-Range Planning,* 29(1), 1996, pp. 38-48.

13. AT&T Corporation, *AT&T 1995 Annual Report*, New York: AT&T Inc., February 11, 1996.

Chapter 5

1. Sandy Berry and Kathryn Britney, "Market Segmentation: Key to Growth in Small Business Banking," *Bank Management*, January/February 1996, pp. 36-41.

2. "Missing the Market," *American Demographics,* December 1989, pp. 16-21, prepared by the staff of *American Demographics.*

3. Walter S. Mossberg, "Apple Introduces Innovative Machine, But Misses Target," *Wall Street Journal,* May 22, 1997, p. B1.

4. Wendell R. Smith, "Product Differentiation and Market Segmentation as Alternative Marketing Strategies," *Journal of Marketing,* July 1956, pp. 3-8, 1956.

5. Y. Datta, "Market Segmentation: An Integrated Framework," *Long-Range Planning,* 29(6), 1996, pp. 797-811.

6. Norton Paley, "Stepping Up Sales," *Sales & Marketing Management,* September 1996, pp. 34-35.

7. For a detailed discussion of business segmentation bases see: Art Weinstein, *Market Segmentation: Using Demographics, Psychographics, and Other Niche Marketing Techniques to Predict Customer Behavior,* Burr Ridge, IL: Irwin Professional Publishing, 1994.

8. For example see: Charles B. Ames and James D. Hlavacek, *Managerial Marketing for Industrial Firms,* New York: Random House, 1984; and Robert R. Reeder, Edward G. Brierty, and Betty H. Reeder, *Industrial Marketing,* Second Edition, Englewood Cliffs, NJ: Prentice-Hall, 1991.

9. Findings in this section were first reported in Art Weinstein, "Market Selection in Technology-Based Industry: Strategic Insights from Executives," in Rajan Varadarajan and Bernard Jaworski (Eds.), *American Marketing Association Winter Educators' Conference,* February 20-23, 1993, Newport Beach, CA, p. 1.

10. David E. Schnedler, "Using Strategic Market Models to Predict Customer Behavior," *Sloan Management Review,* Spring 1996, pp. 85-92.

11. Thomas S. Robertson and Howard Barich, "A Successful Approach to Segmenting Industrial Markets," *Planning Review,* November 1992, pp. 4-11, 48.

12. Andrew Kupfer, "GTE: Son of Internet," *Fortune,* June 23, 1997, pp. 120-122.

13. Melanie Warner, "How to Win Big—Quietly," *Fortune,* November 25, 1996, p. 170.

14. Mimi Whitefield, "Ivax Sells Off IV Unit," *Miami Herald,* May 31, 1997, pp. 1C, 3C.

15. U.S. Office of Management and Budget, *Standard Industrial Classification Manual,* Washington, DC, 1987.

16. James W. McKie, "Market Definition and the SIC Approach," in Franklin M. Fisher (Ed.), *Antitrust and Regulation: Essays in Memory of John J. McGowan,* Cambridge, MA: MIT Press, 1985, pp. 85-100.

17. Thomas V. Bonoma and Benson P. Shapiro, *Segmenting the Industrial Market,* Lexington, MA: Lexington Books, 1983.

Chapter 6

1. Jill Andresky Fraser, "How Many Accountants Does It Take to Change an Industry?," *Inc.,* April 1997, pp. 63-69.

2. Andrew S. Grove, *Only the Paranoid Survive,* New York: Currency/Doubleday, 1996.

3. Derek F. Abell, *Defining the Business: The Starting Point of Strategic Planning,* Englewood Cliffs, NJ: Prentice-Hall, 1980.

4. Derek F. Abell, "Strategic Windows," *Journal of Marketing,* 42, July 1978, pp. 21-26.

5. Peter J. Flatow, "Managing Change: Learning from Motorola," *Marketing News,* July 1, 1996, p. 9.

6. W. Chan Kim and Renee Mauberge, "On the Inside Track," *Financial Times,* April 7, 1997, p. 10.

7. Eryn Brown, "First: Could the Very Best PC Maker Be Dell Computer?," *Fortune,* April 14, 1997, pp. 26-27.

8. Orville C. Walker Jr. and Robert W. Ruekert, "Marketing's Role in the Implementation of Business Strategies: A Critical Review and Conceptual Framework," *Journal of Marketing,* 51, July 1987, pp. 15-33.

9. Art Weinstein, "Market Definition and Redefinition: An Application to Industrial High-Tech Markets," in David W. Stewart and Naufel J. Vilcassim (Eds.), *American Marketing Association Winter Educators' Conference Proceedings,* La Jolla, CA, 1995, pp. 277-284.

10. Luc Rouach, "Marketing for New Technologies: Is Market Research Really Useful for Strategic Marketing in the New Technologies Area?," *Marketing and Research Today,* November 1996, pp. 254-259.

11. Hans Muhlbacher, Angelika Dreher, and Angelika Gabriel-Ritter, "MIPS—Managing Industrial Positioning Strategies," *Industrial Marketing Management,* 23, 1994, pp. 287-294.

Chapter 7

1. Neil Gross, Peter Coy, and Otis Port, "The Technology Paradox: How Companies Can Thrive as Prices Dive," *Business Week,* March 6, 1995, pp. 76-84.

2. Geoffrey R. Brooks, "Defining Market Boundaries," *Strategic Management Journal,* 16, October 1995, pp. 535-549.

3. Alfred M. Pelham and David T. Wilson, "A Longitudinal Study of the Impact of Market Structure, Firm Structure, Strategy, and Market Orientation Culture on Dimensions of Small-Firm Performance," *Journal of the Academy of Marketing Science,* 24, Winter, 1996, pp. 27-43.

4. Jack Reardon and Laurie Reardon, "The Restructuring of the Hospital Services Industry," *Journal of Economic Issues,* 29, December 1995, pp. 1063-1081.

5. Allan D. Shocker, "Competitive Relationships Must Be Viewed from Customer Perspectives," *Marketing Educator,* Fall 1986, pp. 4-5.

6. Hans D. Thorelli, *Strategy + Structure = Performance: The Strategic Planning Imperative,* Bloomington, IN: Indiana University Press, 1977.

7. Frederic Scherer, *Industrial Market Structure and Economic Performance,* Second Edition, Boston: Houghton-Mifflin Company, 1980.

8. Robert F. Lusch and Gene R. Laczniak, "Macroenvironmental Forces, Marketing Strategy and Business Performance: A Futures Research Approach," *Journal of the Academy of Marketing Science,* 17, Fall 1989, pp. 283-295.

9. John M. Vernon, *Market Structure and Industrial Performance: A Review of Statistical Findings,* Boston: Allyn and Bacon Inc., 1972.

10. William E. Cox Jr., "Product Portfolio Strategy, Market Structure, and Performance," in Hans B. Thorelli (Ed.), *Strategy + Structure = Performance: The Strategic Planning Imperative,* Bloomington, IN: Indiana University Press, 1977. Cox noted the lack of conduct and performance measures in previous studies. The research described in this chapter effectively dealt with this concern.

11. Joseph L. Bower and Clayton M. Christiansen, "Disruptive Technologies: Catching the Wave," *Harvard Business Review,* January-February 1995, pp. 43-53.

12. Ajay Kohli and Bernard J. Jaworski, "Market Orientation: The Construct, Research Propositions, and Managerial Implications," *Journal of Marketing,* 54, April 1990, pp. 1-18.

13. John C. Narver and Stanley S. Slater, "The Effect of a Market Orientation on Business Profitability," *Journal of Marketing,* 54, October 1990, pp. 20-35.

14. George S. Day and Prakash Nedungadi, "Managerial Representations of Competitive Advantage," *Journal of Marketing,* 58, April 1994, pp. 31-44.

15. George S. Day and Allan D. Shocker, *Identifying Competitive Product-Market Boundaries,* Report No. 76-112, Cambridge, MA: Marketing Science Institute, 1976.

16. For example, see Derek F. Abell, *Defining the Business: The Starting Point of Strategic Planning,* Englewood Cliffs, NJ: Prentice-Hall, 1980; George S. Day, "Strategic Market Analysis and Definition: An Integrated Approach," *Strategic Management Journal,* 2, May 1981, pp. 281-299; Ira Horowitz, "Market Definition, Market Power, and Potential Competition," *Quarterly Review of Economics and Business,* 22, Autumn 1982, pp. 23-42; and Allan D. Shocker, David W. Stewart, and Anthony J. Zahorik, "Determining the Competitive Structure of Product-Markets: Practices, Issues, and Suggestions," *Journal of Managerial Issues,* 2, Summer 1990, pp. 127-159.

17. Battelle Technology Group, "The List: Wonders of Tomorrow," *Business Week,* March 6, 1995, p. 6.

18. Hubert Gatignon and Jean-Marc Xuereb, "Strategic Orientation of the Firm and New Product Performance," *Journal of Marketing Research,* 34, February 1997, pp. 77-90.

19. David Poppe, "A Speedy Turnaround," *Miami Herald,* December 2, 1996, p. 14T.

20. This approach is described in Karl G. Joreskog and Dag Sorbom, *LISREL 6: Analysis of Linear Structural Relationships, Fourth Edition,* Uppsala, Sweden: University of Uppsala. SPSS Inc., Chicago, also has information available on how to use LISREL methodology.

21. Complete discussion on this methodology is provided in Arthur T. Weinstein, *Market Definition in Industrial Technology Markets,* Miami: Florida International University, PhD dissertation, 1991.

22. Frederick E. Webster Jr., "The Rediscovery of the Marketing Concept," *Business Horizons,* 31, May-June 1988, pp. 29-39.

23. Susan A. Mohrman and Mary Ann Von Glinow, "High Technology Organizations," *Journal of Engineering and Technology Management,* 6, May 1990, pp. 261-280.

24. Parry M. Norling, "Industrial Research Institute's Annual R & D Trends Forecast," *Research Technology Management,* January-February 1995, pp. 14-16.

25. Microsoft Corporation, *Microsoft 1995 Annual Report,* Redmond, WA: Microsoft Corporation, 1995, p. 17.

26. Herbert M. Blalock Jr., *Conceptualization and Measurement in the Social Sciences,* Beverly Hills, CA: Sage Publications, 1982.

PART III: MARKET REDEFINITION: FINDING STRATEGIC ADVANTAGE

Chapter 8

1. Gary Hamel, "Killer Strategies That Make Shareholders Rich," *Fortune,* June 23, 1997, pp. 70-84.

2. Philip Kotler, *Marketing Management: Analysis, Planning, Implementation, and Control,* Eighth Edition, Englewood Cliffs, NJ: Prentice-Hall, 1994.

3. Gary Hamel and C. K. Prahalad, "Seeing the Future First," *Fortune,* September 5, 1994, pp. 64-67, 70.

4. Anat Bird and Peter Louderback, "Creating a Profitable Customer Relationship Using Segmentation Data," *Bankers Magazine,* November/December 1995, pp. 16-22.

5. Sara Q. Duffy, "Do Competitive Hospitals Really Adopt Technology Faster? An Analysis of the Influence of Alternative Relevant Market Definitions," *Eastern Economic Journal,* 18, Spring 1992, pp. 187-208.

6. Fred Wiersama, *Customer Intimacy: Pick Your Partners, Shape Your Culture, Win Together,* Santa Monica, CA: Knowledge Exchange, 1996.

7. Dan Thomas, "Strategy: What's Your Business," *Success,* July/August 1994, p. 13.

8. I thank Gary Korenjel for providing this example, personal communication, April 24, 1997.

Chapter 9

1. Adam M. Brandenburger and Barry J. Nalebuff, *Coopetition,* New York: Currency/Doubleday, 1996.

2. C. K. Prahalad and Gary Hamel, "The Core Competence of the Corporation," *Harvard Business Review,* May-June 1990, pp. 79-91.

3. Moshe Givon, "Variety Seeking, Market Partitioning, and Segmentation," *International Journal of Research in Marketing,* 2, 1985, pp. 117-127.

4. Tom Dillon, "The Triumph of Creativity Over Communication," *Journal of Advertising,* 4(3), 1975, pp. 15-18.

5. Richard Cross, "For Interactive Action, Just Slip Me a Disk," *Direct Marketing,* 59, October 1996, pp. 56-59.

6. G. W. Robinson, "Technology Foresight—The Future for IT," *Long Range Planning,* 29(2), pp. 232-238.

7. Joseph Morone, *Winning in High-Tech Markets: The Role of General Management,* Boston: Harvard Business School Press, 1993.

8. Michael A. Verespej, "The R & D Challenge: Getting It Out of the Lab," *Industry Week,* May 4, 1987, pp. 32-36.

9. Ravi S. Achrol, "Evolution of the Marketing Organization: New Forms for Turbulent Environments," *Journal of Marketing,* 55, October 1991, pp. 77-93.

10. Axel Johne, "Listening to the Voice of the Market," *International Marketing Review,* 11(1), 1994, pp. 47-59.

11. Art Weinstein, "Market Definition in Technology-Based Industry: A Comparative Study of Small Versus Nonsmall Companies," *Journal of Small Business Management,* October 1994, pp. 28-36.

12. Nancy S. Dorfman, *Innovation and Market Structure: Lessons from the Computer and Semiconductor Industries,* Cambridge, MA: Ballinger Publishing Company, 1987.

13. Joseph A. Schumpeter, *Capitalism, Socialism, and Democracy,* Third Edition, New York: Harper & Brothers, 1950.

14. Michael Robert, "Finding Your Strategic Heartbeat," *Journal of Business Strategy,* 15, May-June 1994, pp. 17-22.

15. Bruce D. Henderson, "The Anatomy of Competition," *Journal of Marketing,* 47, Spring 1983, pp. 7-11.

16. Hervé Mathe and Teo Forcht Dagi, "Harnessing Technology in Global Service Businesses," *Long-Range Planning,* 29(4), 1996, pp. 449-461.

17. Warnock Davies and Kathleen E. Brush, "High-Tech Industry Marketing: The Elements of a Sophisticated Global Strategy," *Industrial Marketing Management,* 26, 1997, pp. 1-13.

18. "Trends in U.S. Electronics," *Miami Herald Business Monday,* October 29, 1990, p. 15.

19. Daniel Kadlec, "Companies Loosen Their Belts Again," *USA Today,* August 31, 1995, p. 3B.

20. P. Rajan Varadarajan, "Marketing's Contribution to Strategy: A View from a Different Looking Glass," *Journal of the Academy of Marketing Science,* 20, Fall 1992, pp. 335-343.

21. Associated Press, "Monsanto to Shed Chemicals Business," *USA Today*, December 10, 1996, p. 3B.

22. Jonathan Marshall, "Texas Instruments Betting on Digital Signal Processor Chips," *Miami Herald Business Monday*, July 14, 1997, p. 7BB.

23. "Merger Mania," *Journal of Business Strategy*, 18, March/April 1997, p. 64.

24. Johnson & Johnson, *Johnson & Johnson Mid-Year Report*, New Brunswick, NJ: Johnson & Johnson, 1997, p. 14.

25. John R. Harbison and Peter Pekar Jr., "Strategic Togetherness," *Across the Board*, 34, February 1997, pp. 56-57.

26. Charles T. Saldarini, "Fast Forward on the Sales Force: Where Do We Go from Here?," *Medical Marketing & Media*, 31, September 1996, pp. 52-56.

27. William E. Jackson III, "Is the Market Well Defined in Bank Merger and Acquisition Analysis?," *The Review of Economics and Statistics*, 1992, pp. 655-661.

Chapter 10

1. Art Weinstein, "Market Definition: Strategies and Guidelines for Technology Executives," *Competitive Intelligence Review*, 6(3), 1995, pp. 52-57.

2. William Patalon III, "Digital Difficulty: Kodak Division Faces Growing Pains," *USA Today*, July 31, 1997, p. 7B.

3. James A. Rice, Richard S. Slack, and Pamela A. Garside, "Hospitals Can Learn Valuable Marketing Strategies from Hotels," *Hospitals*, 55, November 16, 1981, pp. 95-99.

4. Kamran Kashani, "Marketing Futures: Priorities for a Turbulent Environment," *Long-Range Planning*, 28(4), 1995, pp. 87-98.

5. Sandra Vandermerwe, *The Eleventh Commandment: Transforming to Own Customers*, Chichester, England: John Wiley & Sons, Ltd., 1996.

6. Robert Smallwood, "Reengineering," *Inform*, October 1996, p. 64.

7. The following marketing texts were consulted: David W. Cravens, *Strategic Marketing*, Fifth Edition, Chicago: Irwin, 1997; Subhash C. Jain, *Marketing Planning and Strategy*, Fourth Edition, Cincinnati, OH: Southwestern Publishing Company, 1993; Philip Kotler, *Marketing Management: Analysis, Planning, Implementation, and Control*, Ninth Edition, Upper Saddle River, NJ: Prentice-Hall, 1997; E. Jerome McCarthy and William D. Perrault Jr., *Basic Marketing*, Tenth Edition, Homewood, IL: Irwin, 1990; William M. Pride and O. C. Ferrell, *Marketing: Concepts and Strategies*, Seventh Edition, Boston: Houghton Mifflin Company, 1991.

8. Julia Flynn, "The Biology of Business," *Business Week*, July 14, 1997, p. 11.

PART IV: CASE STUDIES

Chapter 11

1. Stephen Lacy, "Ideas for Prospering in a Changing Market," *Newspaper Research Journal*, Summer 1992, pp. 85.

2. Maili Wolf, "In Search of Market Niches," *Journal of Media Economics,* Spring 1993, pp. 45-51.

3. Rolf Rykken, "Hatching New Products for New Needs," *Presstime,* October 1990, p 20.

4. Chad Rubel, "Don't Stop the Presses Yet: Newspapers Explore Interactive Alternatives, But They're Not Ready to Stop Buying Ink," *Marketing News,* November 21, 1994, pp. 12-13, 16.

5. Robert Linneman and John L. Stanton, *Making Niche Marketing Work: How to Grow Bigger by Acting Smaller,* New York: McGraw-Hill, 1991.

6. Tony Panaccio, "Stop the Presses!," *South Florida Magazine,* October 1994, pp. 64-67, 84.

PART V: APPENDIXES

Appendix A

1. The industry selection process is described in Art Weinstein, "Defining High Technology Markets: An Evaluation and Typology," in Abbass F. Alkhafaji (Ed.), *International Academy of Business Disciplines Proceedings,* Washington, DC, April 2-5, 1992, pp. 776-783.

Appendix B

1. Sidney Schoeffler, "Cross-Sectional Study of Strategy, Structure, and Performance: Aspects of the PIMS Program," in Hans D. Thorelli (Ed.), *Strategy + Structure = Performance: The Strategic Planning Imperative,* Bloomington, IN: Indiana University Press, 1977.

2. J. Paul Peter, "Construct Validity: A Review of Basic Issues and Marketing Practices," *Journal of Marketing Research,* 18, May 1981, pp. 133-145.

3. This is considered acceptable for exploratory research according to Jum C. Nunnally, *Psychometric Theory,* New York: McGraw-Hill, 1978.

Index

Page numbers followed by the letter "t" indicate tables; those followed by the letter "f" indicate figures.

Order Your Own Copy of
This Important Book for Your Personal Library!

DEFINING YOUR MARKET
Winning Strategies for High-Tech, Industrial, and Service Firms

_____ in hardbound at $39.95 (ISBN: 0-7890-0251-5)

_____ in softbound at $29.95 (ISBN: 0-7890-0252-3)

COST OF BOOKS_____

OUTSIDE USA/CANADA/
MEXICO: ADD 20%_____

POSTAGE & HANDLING_____
(US: $3.00 for first book & $1.25
for each additional book)
Outside US: $4.75 for first book
& $1.75 for each additional book)

SUBTOTAL_____

IN CANADA: ADD 7% GST_____

STATE TAX_____
(NY, OH & MN residents, please
add appropriate local sales tax)

FINAL TOTAL_____
(If paying in Canadian funds,
convert using the current
exchange rate. UNESCO
coupons welcome.)

☐ **BILL ME LATER:** ($5 service charge will be added)
(Bill-me option is good on US/Canada/Mexico orders only;
not good to jobbers, wholesalers, or subscription agencies.)

☐ Check here if billing address is different from
shipping address and attach purchase order and
billing address information.

Signature_____

☐ **PAYMENT ENCLOSED: $**_____

☐ **PLEASE CHARGE TO MY CREDIT CARD.**

☐ Visa   ☐ MasterCard   ☐ AmEx   ☐ Discover
☐ Diner's Club
Account # _____

Exp. Date _____

Signature _____

Prices in US dollars and subject to change without notice.

NAME _____

INSTITUTION _____

ADDRESS _____

CITY _____

STATE/ZIP _____

COUNTRY _____ COUNTY (NY residents only) _____

TEL _____ FAX _____

E-MAIL_____
May we use your e-mail address for confirmations and other types of information? ☐ Yes   ☐ No

Order From Your Local Bookstore or Directly From
The Haworth Press, Inc.
10 Alice Street, Binghamton, New York 13904-1580 • USA
TELEPHONE: 1-800-HAWORTH (1-800-429-6784) / Outside US/Canada: (607) 722-5857
FAX: 1-800-895-0582 / Outside US/Canada: (607) 772-6362
E-mail: getinfo@haworthpressinc.com
PLEASE PHOTOCOPY THIS FORM FOR YOUR PERSONAL USE.

BOF96